Poetry Projects
to Make and Do

Poetry Projects
to Make and Do

Edited by Deborah Alma

Nine
Arches
Press

Poetry Projects to Make and Do
Edited by Deborah Alma

ISBN: 978-1-913437-62-6
eISBN: 978-1-913437-63-3

First published November 2023 by:

Nine Arches Press
Unit 14, Sir Frank Whittle Business Centre,
Great Central Way, Rugby.
CV21 3XH
United Kingdom

www.ninearchespress.com

Printed in the United Kingdom on recycled paper by:
Imprint Digital

Nine Arches Press is supported using public funding
by Arts Council England.

Supported using public funding by
**ARTS COUNCIL
ENGLAND**

Contents

PART TWO: Projects for Groups and Creative Collaborations

PART THREE: Projects in Public

Deborah Alma

Introduction:
On Making It Happen

There's an internet meme I came across with a quote from Buddhist teacher, author and nun Pema Chodron set against a wild and stormy Himalayan backdrop.

Let your curiosity be greater than your fear.

I usually find inspirational memes really irritating, but this one got through somehow. As I write this, about to set off towards the mountain of another project that's too big for me, there it was! These words more-or-less sum me up.

First comes the idea, the project, the sense of adventure. This is exciting. It's like falling in love. Something chemical happens in the brain; you're hooked. For me the approach to a new project feels like my approach to a new poem. They have in common a state of receptiveness, playfulness and being open to the most fantastical of possibilities. I have learnt to lean into the idea and start to move in that direction however far-fetched it may seem and begin to have conversations with friends and potential collaborators. Those first steps are significant. Somehow a good idea can then take on a life of its own and a forward momentum. You find you've started something.

For me, this is not the time to look too hard at the possible pitfalls. It's a state of creativity, visualisation and imagination. The reasons not to do this project will come crowding in later. If you write a checklist at this stage, it may get you nowhere and the idea may be abandoned too soon. Don't expect to have everything in place; you don't need to have all the answers to how or even why at this stage. *Delight in disorder*. (Robert Herrick). This attitude of receptivity and flexibility will serve you in good stead once your project starts to come to life and starts to go where it needs to go.

I remember feeling this sense of being taken over by excitement when I came across a 1950's ambulance for sale on eBay back in 2011 and immediately visualised what was to become the long-running Emergency Poet project. Travelling dressed as a doctor, with Nurse Verse and a pharmacy of poetry in pills under the awning; I could see it all in my imagination even as I was bidding in the auction. I think that there was not one person at the time amongst my friends and family who thought that this was a sensible idea. The naysayers are useful however – they may have good and valid points and your answers will test both the idea and your resolve. I must admit to also wanting to prove them wrong. I enjoyed the risk, which was not as risky as it seemed in actual fact. Although I was a low-income single parent and bought it with my overdraft facility, at the same time I knew I could always sell it and get my money back.

For me it was important to have an attitude that I would either 'succeed' or learn something. There was no such thing as failure. To allow oneself to enter this apparently naïve state may not be easy. You may have to let go of a little dignity and stop caring what other people think of you. The vintage ambulance parked outside our house was an agony for my then teenage sons and the neighbours. They had to get used to it. The fact is that most people will think of what you're up to only fleetingly, if at all and get on with their own lives. It doesn't matter. You will be doing what you want to do. This can be a great place of self-actualisation, however small. Your life and your work are becoming the same thing. This I believe is a great achievement. Congratulations!

I seem to have an extreme case of the making-it-happen disease. I grew up in a household where we waited until we had enough money / time / energy to paint the room / go on holiday / move job or house; waiting for all the ducks to line up prettily in a row. Of course, those ducks kept shifting about and nothing got done. I resolved not to be like that. I may have overdone it.

In each project or undertaking, I always and quite early on, consider my fallback position. What's the worst that can happen? If that's not so bad, that's your safety net. My safety net is a very comfortable one involving tea, cake and friends. Your own safety net is always there and knowing it's there will get you through the bad days – a little spring in the net and up you get. The safety net with the ambulance was improving a vintage vehicle with the potential of selling it on if necessary (and in fact when I did eventually sell it, it had gone up in value). Later, and after one unsuccessful Arts Council bid, there was a second attempt and a little bit of funding support to enable me to do things better. Maybe some external funding can be your safety net, although I was determined to do it anyway and I think the Arts Council like to know this about a project.

You will explore new things; you will learn and grow, and learn when to change direction, re-think or do things differently. There can be no failure, only adaptation or growth. You will be altogether more contented and properly yourself in the world. This is an attractive and energetic state and draws towards it people that want to work with you. You will find yourself on an upward spiral; it's still hard work but very rewarding.

Don't confuse this naïve state with ignorance. It can seem that way to people looking-on. It is just seeing the most positive outcome and working towards that. Ignorance is all about not looking and avoiding the problems – don't do that! It's just that the *received wisdoms, the sensible approach, the properly costed, the mature decision* can be a chimera; something hoped for but impossible to achieve. I don't at all mean to advocate recklessness; remember you have always have your safety net; but what have you got to lose? You really have so much to gain.

If your project necessarily involves working with or for others, it makes sense that you are properly part of these communities and then you will have worked with them already and know how they work. I remember when my friend Dr Katie Amiel and I were talking of putting together the poetry anthology *These Are the Hands – Poems from the Heart of the NHS* we had first to find a publisher. We could have approached a large/mainstream publisher with Michael Rosen and the Royal College of General Practitioners on board, but I had worked with my good friend and publisher Nadia Kingsley of Fair Acre Press when editing *#Metoo – Rallying against sexual assault and harassment – a women's poetry anthology* and it had been a great pleasure to work with her. We worked well together, plus she was retraining to become a GP. It felt right.

I'm a firm believer in a kind of karmic attitude to working on projects. I believe that in order to *ask* something of a community you must first have given and given some more. In the world of poetry, this means you buy the books, go to the open mics, read the poems of friends and others, and share their successes, workshops and readings on your social media and more. Only then can you ask. I don't mean this cynically – that you give only in *order* to receive – but that you involve yourself in a community so you work with relationships that are real and authentic. It is not who you know, but *how* you know them. And thank you so much Nadia for both of those books!

When working collaboratively, start from a position of 'I don't *need* anything from you, but what can we do together?' Be open to ideas and suggestions from others, listen really carefully to each other and learn what is realistic to expect from each other in terms of commitment, time and energy. Be prepared to be flexible when people can't do as much as they had hoped.

I also learnt that if people offer to help, always say 'yes'. Someone else's energy, belief and generosity for your project is too valuable to turn down, even if it's hard to accept – there will always be something they can do. If you find it uncomfortable to work alongside someone or to hand over too much control, try asking them to distribute flyers, or help set up a room, or simply to share something on social media. I have learnt that people really do like to be involved.

If you can, surround yourself with people that believe in your project, their confidence will buoy you up when you falter. They may become the place to express any vulnerabilities and uncertainties, may assist with lightening the workload, and can play a crucial role in developing resilience.

* * *

There's plenty of excellent advice in this book on the nuts and bolts of bringing your project to life; Jonathan Davidson's excellent essay advises on how to attract funding, Caleb Parkin reminds us to look after ourselves as creative people in the process, Clare Shaw speaks eloquently of working with vulnerability when working with groups, and Jean Atkin has good advice on making a living as a writer in the community. All of the essays provide ideas, advice and insights, that range from setting up some space and time for yourself to write and think, right through to working with groups in a wide range of settings. You will find inspiration, wisdom and practical solutions and heads-up for the potential pitfalls.

The book is divided into three distinct sections. The first section, Projects Just For You, includes essays for developing and extending your own practice as a poet; these include Jane Burn who writes about the interconnectedness of her visual and written art, Roz Goddard reminding us of how to read mindfully in order to develop our writing practice, and Nina Mingya Powles inspiring us to think about zine-making.

In Part Two, the essays are concerned with working with groups or in collaboration with others; from Casey Bailey asking the question about why collaboration can be so enriching, to Jasmine Gardosi exploring working with musicians, and Pat Edwards on making space for the work of others in some way, whether it's in reviewing or literally making space to hear other poets in a festival or open-mic setting.

The last section of the book is concerned with creating new poetry projects in the public sphere and making a living as a poet in the world; from Jane Commane's essay on taking poetry out into the world, to Jo Bell's essay on setting up residencies, and Degna Stone's guidance on commissions and drawing inspiration in museum and gallery spaces, all of which offer practical advice and ideas. There's plenty more here also on setting up live and touring performances, taking poetry into theatrical spaces, and projects in other more unusual settings such as in healthcare.

Behind and beyond all of this excellent advice are the ideas and will and drive in the first place. This is what will make it happen – *you* – and you are brilliant. I would like this book to be the gentle hand in the small of your back saying '*Go on. Go on. You can do it.*'

ACTIVITY: Small and easy-to-swallow purgatives for writer's block, stimulants for novel ideas & curatives for sluggish blood

Cultivate boredom. A place *between* is essential for new ideas. Take steps to find this space. Is it a short train journey? A coffee shop that's particularly unstimulating? Keep your notebook in your bag or pocket.

Write a few sentences about an experience you had of doing something for the first time that you thought you couldn't do and that now comes pretty easily to you, e.g. riding a bike, using a computer, a new mobile phone.

Identify what's blocking your writing – address a curse in its name. Write the curse in red ink and bury it in the garden or in a plant pot.

Have you ever entered a house or room when you shouldn't have? Write about the experience. Describe the room in minute detail, as well as your feelings. What did you find?

Write a list (no need to be definitive) of ten books you have loved or that have some meaning to for you in some way. By each book, write three words you'd use to describe it, or which take you to the time of reading. Find connections with what you have written.

Write a poem or piece of writing infused with a colour, without actually naming the colour. See if you can make it painterly, e.g. an imaginative walk encountering a frog, a fern curling, a glass of lime juice.

If you could take a week outside of your everyday life to do nothing but read and write, where would you go? Describe your week. What do you need?

Sit still and quiet, and listen. Listen and identify each of the sounds you can hear. Write them down; the pipes rushing with water, a passing car, a floorboard thud from another flat. Keep going until you come upon a sound that you can't identify. What might it be?

Part One

Projects Just For You

Roz Goddard

Netting the Golden Fish:
Reading Like a Poet

When I was a teenager in the seventies filling notebooks with outpourings of dark feelings and notions, my father paid good money to have my poems published. I spotted a small ad in the *Daily Mirror* asking poets to submit their best poems for inclusion in an anthology – which I duly did. The reply was encouragingly swift and let me know I was the new Sylvia Plath and could I send £40 for inclusion in the anthology? My dad paid up. The anthology, when it arrived, was a green exercise book with my poems squashed toward the bottom of page eighty-three. I've never forgotten the disappointed surprise tinged with shame – it woke me up somewhat. I knew nothing then. I didn't read poetry. Why bother? I was a genius. I like to think Dad's money wasn't wasted – I read lots of poetry now, some of which are fully accessible in the library of my heart.

My long-time friend and poet Jonathan Davidson is an advocate of reading poems slowly, giving them their due attention, often returning to them over a period of years. On a recent walk, he produced from his wallet a fragile and many-times folded copy of the W. S. Graham poem 'Johann Joachim Quantz's Five Lessons' – a poem that has been a companion to him for over thirty years: "when solace is required, it is this little piece of genius that I reach for."

In his recently published essay 'The Slow Poetry Movement' (Redden Press, 2023), he advocates experiencing "as deeply as possible the pleasures and illuminations that can unfold from spending time with a poem". I agree.

I can remember the moment I came across Katherine Mansfield's poem 'Pulmonary Tuberculosis'. It felt like I'd been waiting for it my whole life – an 'Oh, I see' moment. I seemed to have gone beyond my initial comprehension of the poem – an intellectual understanding if you like – to access a deeper resonance that tapped into an experience of illness I instinctively knew could open significant doors to new ways of thinking for me.

Mansfield suffered from pulmonary tuberculosis for much of her life and was regularly treated in sanatoriums for her illness. Here's the poem:

Pulmonary Tuberculosis

The man in the room next to mine has the same complaint as I. When I wake in the night I hear him turning. And then he coughs. And I cough. And after a silence I cough. And he coughs again. This goes on for a long time. Until I feel we are like two roosters calling to each other at a false dawn. From far-away hidden farms.

Since I was young, I've been deeply affected by illness. My mother was gravely ill when I was a child and I remember that painful, twilight time of not knowing whether she would live or die. During those days of my mother's illness, reading became a sanctuary in the uncertainty and sadness. I read Johanna Spyri's *Heidi* over and over, finding thrill and solace in a child's life on the mountainside under the big, open sky – a fantasy landscape far from my Black Country street with its booming power forges and mysterious warehouses. The stoicism and beauty of the Mansfield poem appeals to me: the scene, the stuckness of two people in illness – together but separate. They are fellow travellers communicating beyond words. It illustrates the tenderness and compassion that can be felt when witnessing the pain of others – it's a poem about our human predicament and the choices we have in how we deal with sorrow and helplessness. Mansfield is an observer of her experience as well as being in it.

I was diagnosed with breast cancer at the end of 2020 and, during that time of deep anxiety, I returned to this poem to remind myself that I'm not alone and also that I have a choice about how I view and assimilate my experience.

If I can bear to be with the pain of diagnosis, what it might mean for my future, be tender with the experience – it could be helpful.

Our reading choices are always telling us something about where we're at in our lives. Currently my addiction to soft-boiled crime fiction is telling me I'm feeling overwhelmed in my life and need to carve out some time to enter the world of forensic archaeology, sand dunes and peril that isn't my own. I'm pulled along by the propulsive narrative, lightly-sketched characters and a desire for certainty my own life can't deliver. If I reflect on my reading habits – it always brings me closer to myself; getting closer to myself opens up my choices about how I live – I'm observing rather than simply consuming.

I often lead poetry writing workshops and begin the session with a period of mindful reading practice – an opportunity to read in silence together, uninterrupted in a conducive space. Maybe you'd like to try it for twenty minutes? Here goes: Select a book pretty much at random from your shelf. Sit down somewhere comfy and, as you read, become aware of how you're reading. This might include noting the pace you read: fast or slow? Is the text causing a particular response? Maybe it's speaking deeply to you or causing resistance. Notice what's resonating. Stay with the words or phrases, perhaps writing down what you find interesting. Is the text speaking deeply to you? What's it saying? How does it make you feel?

It's an instructive exercise as it's rare to examine how we read rather than what we're reading. I was recently reading a poet new to me and was surprised by how resistant I was to the work: it was thematically challenging and formally difficult, and my attention regularly drifted off. During a pause, I wondered how this might be a richer experience for me – the answer was to give the poetry a better quality of attention; my mind was dismissing the work too soon.

I often follow the mindful reading session with a led meditation which you'll find in the appendix – it seems to be a good companion to the sense of awareness that's been developed from mindful reading. As a practising Buddhist, I meditate regularly. Meditation has been described as the "art of being with oneself" or as Alan Watts has written "being in the eternal flow". It's a stillness practice that brings me back to myself by deepening my awareness of feelings, emotions and thoughts – like catching a net of golden fish as they swim up. What I discover can be surprising, difficult, beautiful. I've found that sitting still over a period of time opens up new spaces in my heart and mind into which diverse ideas have the opportunity to incubate and flower – in other words, the ideal conditions for new poems to emerge.

I'm currently fascinated by Zuihitsu, a form of Japanese poetry that feels like a poetic partner to meditation. In her 2006 collection of poems, *The Narrow Road to the Interior*, Kimiko Hahn muses on its definition. She looks for something that comes close to "a sense of disorder that feels so integral" and finds Donald Keene's definition that, with its urgency and instinctual composition, Zuihitsu "follows the impulse of the brush".

I wanted to explore the idea of following the 'impulse of the pen'. Those of us who have attended writing workshops over the years will be familiar with the automatic writing 'killing the white' or freewriting exercise designed to subvert the judging mind and produce a more natural flow of writing. I'm discovering in my own writing that by going deeper into an image or feeling, a rich flow of fragments and juxtapositions start to shine that seem to come from a place between the heart and the belly – a flow around a theme combined with a surprising tone that I'm enjoying.

Meditation and silence have helped me conceive and approach a different way of writing – not an intellectual, thought-through process but rather an instinctive response to the deepest rivers of my feelings and experience, being alive to what it means to be alive in all its complexity and how I might express that creatively.

Recently, I've returned to keeping a journal as a way of systematically accessing my thoughts and feelings – trying to truthfully record how I feel about the heartache and joys of my life. I returned to Marion Milner's *A Life of One's Own*, first published in 1934, in which she discovers that keeping a journal enables her to "plunge into the deeper waters of the mind … suggesting creatures whose ways I did not know."

Her journal becomes a deep, and faithful record of her loves, hates and fears. Writing a journal seems to be a way of subverting the thinking mind, illuminating what I don't know about myself in surprising and exhilarating ways.

After all, writing poetry is not a rational pursuit. I find thinking to be the enemy of writing poetry – particularly in the drafting stage. I recently shared a manuscript in progress with my editor; she enjoyed a section that had been written full pelt, Zuihitsu-style from the belly. I like it too, it's full of blood and energy.

I came across a YouTube video of poet Ocean Vuong talking about his approach to teaching (he's Professor of Creative Writing at NYU). He "doesn't centre criticism", rather the first five weeks in an Ocean Vuong poetry workshop is about encouraging students to "name the work", to "get to know the ambition". He's interested in getting students to explore their writing territories to understand what the seabed of their deepest pulls and concerns are: "students discover the effects of their intent". It seems to me that beginning to understand and own our obsessions and experiences is a dazzling gift we can give to ourselves. After a deeply traumatic experience, in which he nearly died, the poet

David Whyte noticed how his voice had changed:

> It was no longer up in my throat, ready to be given away and please others so readily. It settled in my stomach along with my breath ... my voice could suddenly allow the presence of darker hidden energies I had previously left unexplored.

Where does reading feature in the "transcendental joy of composition", as Don Paterson puts it? I recently listed my reading research for a sequence of poems I'm writing: *Standing in the Forest of Being Alive* (Katie Farris), the Rijksmuseum Vermeer catalogue, astrophotography, orchards, river behaviour, wild horses, characters in *Tess of the D'Urbervilles*, the manufacture of gold jewellery. The diversity of my sources seems to echo an intangible energy in my body and mind whose alchemy produces the poem draft – in other words, I don't know what's going on. What I do know is the dropping in of text, fragments, images and memories is exciting, but I'm clueless about where the poem will end up. David Whyte again:

> ... our ability to respond creatively, whether at our desks or on the yet unwritten page, depends on our ability to live with the unexplored territory of silence.

Wait, wait.

Years ago, I had a rejection from a poetry magazine. The editor liked the beginning of the poem yet found the end "rather striven for". I didn't understand then that life can't be neatly tied up. I do now.

When I read a wonderful poem, it feels like blue ink has dissolved in a pool of clear water – the ripples carry on right to the edge then beyond the pond to a deeper place of understanding that gives me a unique glimpse of what it means to be alive.

ACTIVITY: Writing from the openness

Just sitting (10–15 mins).

Find a spot where you can be undisturbed for a time. Set yourself up in a comfortable position: sit on a chair or lie down on the floor or bed, and maybe cover yourself lightly with a blanket so you are warm enough. Give yourself the opportunity for this a period of stillness. Clench your fists really tight for a few moments then let go completely and relax back.

Stillness gives the body and mind an opportunity to settle. It allows us to step out of the zone of doing and into a space where simply being with what arises in our experience comes to the fore. We can witness the rhythm of our breath however it is, without interference.

Watch thoughts come and go – meditation is not about banishing your mind of thoughts. Scan your body for sensations of warmth, pleasure, pain – whatever's there. Simply be with it without judgement.

At the end of the meditation, gently rise, noticing how your body and mind have responded to the stillness.

If you feel like writing, perhaps journal in a free and loose style about what arose for you.

Works Cited:

Katherine Mansfield, 'Pulmonary Tuberculosis': *The Penguin Book of the Prose Poem*, Ed. Jeremy Noel-Tod, (Penguin, 2018)

David Whyte, *The Heart Aroused: Poetry and the Preservation of the Soul in Corporate America* (Doubleday, 1994)

Ocean Vuong on YouTube 'My Vulnerability is my Power': https://www.youtube.com/watch?v=u5NuCrAkjGw

Joanna Field; Marion Milner, *A Life of One's Own* (Virago Press, 1986).

Nina Mingya Powles

Paper Journeys:
Making Poetry Zines

I held my gaze on the horizon as the minibus sped through the desert. The bright white mountain range parallel to the highway sometimes appeared closer, then further away. My boyfriend, who I was travelling with, tapped my shoulder to look at the landscape on the other side of the road and I gasped: rows and rows of distant turbines, sunlight flashing on their white blades as they turned in unison. I had felt the raw wind of the desert; my cheeks still stung from it. I opened my phone camera and pointed it out the window at the sea of windmills, but the lens barely captured their outlines.

We had met just a few months earlier in Shanghai, where we were both living, and things between us had quickly intensified. In less than six weeks, we were both due to leave the city for our respective home countries, Aotearoa and the UK. We didn't know what would happen next, only that we ought to go somewhere together. Xinjiang was a place neither of us had been, and was about as far away from ordinary life as we could get.

We had driven an hour from the city of Kashgar in China's western Xinjiang Province, near the mountainous borders of Kyrgyzstan and Tajikistan. I glanced at the pulsing blue dot on the map on my phone and wondered if this was the farthest I'd ever been from the ocean.

It was 2017, and the full extent of the Chinese Communist Party's internment camps across the region was not yet known, though Kashgar in particular had seen a steadily growing military presence for several decades. I knew this, and yet the sight of heavily armoured vehicles and armed police dotted around what otherwise felt like a quiet and picturesque old city still shocked me. I was conscious that they watched us, but only out of curiosity; we were not locals and therefore not deemed a threat. Once we were stopped by a military policeman and asked – not threateningly, though he had an automatic rifle slung over his shoulder – why on earth we'd choose to visit 'such a dangerous place.'

I was overwhelmed with the feeling of needing to remember everything we did and saw, to capture the entire trip before it slipped away – before everything changed. My camera roll was filled with pictures of desert structures and market stalls and clouds of purple bougainvillea. As I always did, I wrote down lists of images in my notebook:

> *blue mosaic tiles & tall sunflowers*
> *red tomato the size of a heart*
> *baked lamb dumplings*
> *the smell of dried apricots*

In the days after returning home, as my last day in the city came closer, I decided to make a new zine. I didn't know who it was for: perhaps just for me. It would contain poem fragments, lists and images from the trip. Physical proof that all this really happened: the turbines, the mountain light, the blue glacial lake, his skin and mine. A poetry zine is something you can put together quickly – a poem object you can create yourself with little more than a few sheets of paper.

Much like a poem, a zine can be almost anything you want it to be. At its heart, a zine is a DIY publication of some kind, usually hand-folded and printed in small quantities. My first zines were poetry zines, but categories are flexible in the world of zines. You could make a travel zine, a photography zine, a protest zine, or something that's all three. It could have drawings or collages or pictures; it could be long or short, handwritten or typed. Zinemaking, for me, lies somewhere in the exciting generative space between crafting poetry and journaling. When away from home, it's given me a creative space to reflect. What does it mean to feel rooted in a place where I'm really a visitor? What does it mean to be a tourist in a country where locals cannot criticise their own government freely?

I copied and pasted a few landscape pictures I'd taken on my phone and digitally recoloured them in pale blue – something close to the colour of the sky and the surface of the high-altitude lake where we had stood. I scanned sections of pages from my notebook and cut them up with scissors. I typed up some lines I had written in my notebook, printed them out and placed them on top of the mountains.

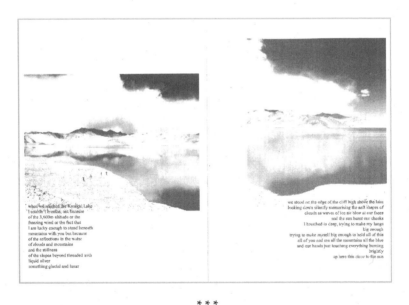

* * *

The first zine I ever made was a booklet of ghost poems titled *(auto)biography of a ghost*. I secretly printed twenty copies in the photocopying room of the creative writing department. On the cover was a grainy black-and-white picture of a shadowy stairwell. I kept making poetry zines, and set up a little stall at my local annual zinefest. In Shanghai, I frequented my university's campus print shop, where you dropped coins into a bucket next to the technician's desk. While other students rushed to print copies of dissertations and exam papers, no one raised an eyebrow at my strange erasure poem printouts.

I also have a stack of notebooks from the eighteen months I lived as a student in Shanghai. Rather than diary entries, they are full of lists, recipes and images. Occasionally I taped train tickets and boarding passes inside, along with mini Polaroids taken with my blue Instax camera. This habit of recording and cataloguing my life only really started when I left my home country, and was perhaps fuelled by the many cheap and cavernous stationery stores close to campus where rows of fresh candy-coloured notebooks of all sizes and varieties greeted me upon entering.

I took my notebook everywhere I went – something I rarely do nowadays. I was often eating alone, which meant I often sat at a table by the window with a bowl of noodles and my notebook, making lists. Lists of Chinese characters to practise, lists of potential poem titles, lists of colours in the sky, lists of recurring dreams. On the crowded subway, I made notes on my phone of things I'd seen, places where I'd stopped to eat. Many of these lists, or fragments of them, later found their way into my first published poems.

What was it about leaving home that turned me into a note-taker? I was at the beginning of something, but I didn't know what. I was living for the first time in two languages. I was overwhelmed by my new surroundings, all the colours and smells and tastes. After my daily Chinese classes, I wrote out sets of characters twenty times each, trying and mostly failing to commit them to muscle memory. I was playing with different forms, both poetic and linguistic. I was learning what my own creative process might look like. I can see now that my language learning was entangled with my zinemaking; at the same time as I cut up squares of paper into vocabulary flashcards, I was cutting scraps of calligraphy paper to fold into mini zines.

Zinemaking reminds me that poetry is physical. It's a way to test out ideas, to try new things and allow myself to get lost in the meditative act of folding and stapling paper, of cutting out words and gluing lines together to make something new.

* * *

It took at least a day and night for me to grow accustomed to the quiet. From our flat near Hampstead Heath in London you could hear owls and teenagers whooping through the night; here in rural Scotland, the only sound was rain falling faintly on the skylight of the cottage. A small art gallery in Dumfriesshire had invited me for a week-long writing residency, and I found myself alone for the first time in many months. I wasn't sure what I had come here to write, or if I'd be able to write at all. But I could make a zine. I could make a small poem object that hadn't existed in the world before, and that would be enough.

The walk from my cottage to the gallery took thirty minutes each morning and evening. It was a mossy walk along a country lane lined with damp stone walls. Tiny ferns grew in the gaps in the stones and a spongy layer of moss enveloped all the branches. In some places the moss was so thick it pulled away from the surface of the bark like a heavy knitted garment. Each morning when I reached the gallery I was out of breath and my fingers were cold. In the evening when I got back to the cottage I felt tired from the effort of trying to generate creative energy. I made myself a bowl of instant noodles with a soft-boiled egg and a teaspoon of Laoganma chilli oil on top – I'd brought a few packets of noodles and a pottle of chilli oil with me from London – and sat down to watch a Netflix documentary about volcanic eruptions as the sky darkened outside the windows.

That night I had strange dreams involving lava deposits and moving islands. Tina, the gallery director, had given me a tourist leaflet with a map of the local area. I began cutting up the map along the blue lines that marked rivers and streams, creating a series of curved shapes. Using the office inkjet printer, I printed a picture of stones I had taken that morning and cut out a rough shape of a volcano. I folded a single sheet of A4 paper into a mini zine and arranged the cut shapes across it. I tried not to overthink their composition, instead being led by lines and shapes and blank space.

moss & pink stone walk is a mini zine documenting my walks around Dumfriesshire and my week spent in the stone cottage. I printed it on lilac office paper and folded it using a ruler to press the corners. Cutting up shapes and words to make poems was a liberating and calming process, and making something so specific to this particular time and place freed myself up to start writing again about other things. I knew this was a zine I'd only give to a handful of people, which made me feel free to experiment and not worry about crafting something too polished. The unfinished, imperfect nature of zines is what I love most about them.

Like submerging myself in cold water, being in a new place often reinvigorates my creative self. But since moving countries several times in my life, the distinction between feeling *at home* and *away from home* has become blurred. Making zines and writing poems has helped me retrace these journeys in memory and given me a space to consider the many smaller, more ordinary journeys that make up my everyday life. Moving through the city, hours spent in the garden at dusk, my weekly swims, the movements of my body around the kitchen. Whenever I am stuck and don't know how to begin, I pick up a blank sheet of paper, fold it in half, and fold it in half again.

ACTIVITY: Make a mini poetry zine

To begin filling in the pages of your mini poetry zine, think of a memorable journey you have made. The journey could be big or small: a regular walking route, a long car trip, or a plane journey across the sea.

On the title page of your zine, draw a line resembling this journey as if you were sketching a quick map for someone. It might be a curved line to represent a transcontinental plane trip, or a loop representing your morning walk.

Document this journey by writing one or two sentences on each inside page of your zine. Spend only a minute or two on each page. Give your words lots of space. Pay attention to the senses: what textures can you feel underfoot? What interesting noises and smells are there? What are some memorable colours from the journey? Think of this more of a note-taking exercise rather than writing lines of poetry. Include further drawings or doodles if you wish.

1. Take a sheet of A4 paper.
Fold the sheet in half lengthways.

2. Fold it in half again, like this:

3. Fold it in half one more time.

4. Open out the sheet of paper.
It should be folded into 8 sections, like this:

5. With scissors, carefully cut into the middle fold.

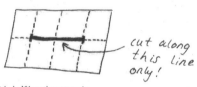

cut along this line only!

6. Fold the sheet in half lengthways again
Open up the centre so you have a cube shape.

7. Flatten it to make the edges meet.

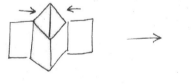

8. Flatten it into the shape of a little book!

Mini zine

Sophie Herxheimer

On Interplay: Image, Language, and Sound
"Listen to my poem like you listen to the rain"
(Octavio Paz)

There are so many approaches to making poems, and sometimes rather limiting labels for the way these might be categorised. You might hear of an *experimental* press, or a *spoken word artist*, or an *established* poet for example, and these words (in a world of words) can immediately suggest a separating out of skill sets, interests, techniques. In art too, people are often looking to categorise. Are you an *emerging* artist? Do you use *watercolours*? Do you *illustrate* your poems? Perhaps your work is more *conceptual*? Some of the labels are to do with *selling* the work, or *buying* into it. Our twisted economy! How to make a living from art is a mystery I cannot answer, I can only report my finding that the wider my skill set is, the more commissions I get, and that having a degree of versatility is a small price to pay for giving people a headache with uncategorisability!

So, I don't see a separation between the techniques I use to communicate. It might be drawing, writing or collage, it might involve collaboration, performance or print. Some ideas call for ink, others for video. I try to ask myself "what is needed here? In what way can I respond?" And that isn't always to a brief, sometimes it is to the personal situation that I find myself in, and I need to just write, or just draw, until I have uncovered something of the current bother or preoccupation. I go into each project or poem in the spirit of what Keats termed *negative capability*. As in the title of one of the old Russian fairy tales: *Go I Know not Whither, and Bring Back I Know not What*. The main hurdle is to get going, to gather one's nerve. I cajole and bribe my petulant inner

36

artist-child with biscuits – and nice paints or scraps of torn paper. She loves this sort of thing, yes, she lives to play.

I trained in visual art, but always had one foot in poetry, stories and books. My paintings often contained (and still do contain) words, there were times when the titles got so big they nudged the images off the canvases. Image making is image making, whether you paint, write poems or direct films really. If you don't believe me, ask William Blake, ask Akira Kurosawa, ask Emily Dickinson!

In this essay I hope to show how poetry and art are inextricably interwoven in my work and in the projects that I undertake, and how in retrospect it looks simple, even to me, but how when one is in the middle it often feels like endless (unpaid, hopeless) chaos and experiment.

Example 1. My first collection, *Velkom to Inklandt:* sounds sprout images

I had bought a place on Kathryn Maris' poetry class with a barter: she swapped me her weekly wisdom for a pair of screenprints I'd made in ghost collaboration with Rosemary Tonks. Kathryn gave our group thought-provoking poetry homework at the end of each session, and the week that set me off on this sequence was particularly impossible. The assignment was: *write a poem in an accent or a dialect.* I was embarrassed to even consider the idea, worrying about whose voice I could snaffle without making a patronising blunder. I began to comb through my memories of growing up in this city that is almost entirely constructed out of accents and dialects. I thought of the Irish navvies escaping the potato famine who likely built the house I live in. My street neighbours from the Caribbean, West Africa, Wales … the Lithuanian guy and his Chinese mate who just fixed the bathroom. All the languages, all the immigrants I hear every day. Incantations of home that help to make me feel at home. Then, of course, my dad occurred to me, he had come here aged 12, and done all in his power to sound completely English, quite posh to boot. And his refugee parents, with their strong German accents and idioms. I remembered my grandmother telling me about her surprise at being addressed as 'love' by a bus conductor when she had recently arrived in 1938. So I wrote a sonnet in her borrowed voice, recounting that story. Back in class, Kathryn got me to read it twice, even suggested it might be 'a keeper'.

London

Not zo mainy Dais zinz ve arrivink.
Zis grey iss like Bearlin, zis same grey Day
ve hef. Zis norzern Vezzer, oont ze demp Street.
A biet off Rain voant hurt, vill help ze Treez
on zis Hempstet Heese ve see in Fekt.
Vy shootd I mind zat?

I try viz ze Busses, Herr Kondooktor eskink
me... for vot? I don't eckzectly remempber;
Fess plees? To him, my Penny I hent ofa -
He notdz viz a keint Smile – *Fanks Luv!*
He sez. Oh! I em his Luff – turns Hentell
on Machine, out kurls a Tikett.

Zis is ven I know zat here to settle iss OK. Zis
City vill be Home, verr eefen on ze Buss is Luff.

A couple of poet friends really inkurritcht me to keep going and write more in 'Liesl's' voice. So slowly, as the right subjects appeared to me, as I wandered about my richly layered city, as ever taking my ghosts in my pocket, I wrote. Many poems came, and I loved performing them. So that audiences could enjoy the phonetics of the writing, and the look of the Inklisch, I blew up photocopies of the text to A0 size and used these huge sheets of paper as props, often getting a taller member of the audience to help me hold them up. I loved dropping these giant pieces of paper onto the floor as a last line hit the air. It was doubly percussive. As the crumpled paper pile I stood in got bigger, the whole thing got funnier, sharpened by contrast: myself, a middle-aged woman dressed up to the (ja-und-)neins, declaiming poems of domesticity and exile from a nest of rubbish. There was a whiff of Kurt Schwitters' Merzbau, and a sense of being a cog in the long-running machine of a European absurdist tradition. Not only was revivifying a version of my granny in our shared London a comfort, it also helped me process some of my fury over Brexit. It was one of these massive performance photocopies that steered these poems into a book.

A woman called Aurea Carpenter had seen and liked a window display that I'd made for National Poetry Day in the window of the LRB bookshop. The theme that year was messages, and I'd arranged a display of books and pamphlets by poets I admired, and then around and amongst them displayed and hung up many various-sized ink drawings of people and animals whispering, reading and shouting to each other. Aurea asked the bookshop if they knew how to get hold of me, because she wanted to buy one of the drawings. She emailed, and I invited her to come round and rummage through my piles of drawings and prints, and I'd make us some lunch. While I was stirring the soup downstairs I heard a shout from the studio, *Sophie, what's this?* She was staring at some giant poems in Inklisch that I'd left draped over the big canvases. *Will you read one to me?* (Vell, vot you sink I sett? Off kors I rett to her zeze Poems.)

She bought a drawing, and a few weeks later, wrote again. It transpired that Aurea was one half of small publisher, Short Books. Their editor, William Pimlott, was studying for a PhD in Yiddish Studies, and loved what I was doing with these poems. Would I come and meet her in town, and please could I bring another screen print she'd seen online.

When she proposed that Short Books would like to publish my 'granny poems', I was bowled over. She asked what illustrations I thought would work with them. *They don't need illustrations,*

I snapped, *they're already visual!* She was so disappointed she forgot to put the nice cake she'd ordered in her mouth. It just sat on the end of her fork, trembling in sugared dismay. The next day her partner at Short Books, Rebecca Nicolson, invited me to come and see her. *Bring your artwork with you, I'd love to see some,* she said. After she'd had a good shuffle through my portfolio, looking interested, asking questions, she said: *When you've decided what pictures you want to make for the Inklisch book, let me know. As soon as possible please.*

They'd trapped me in a pincer movement! She added: *Admit it would be a waste having a book by you without your art in it.* Luckily at dawn the next day I awoke with the words **cut out domestic objects** stamped upon my forehead. My grandmother's rather hairy striped upholstered armchair had sprung into my mind in my sleep – along with her kitchen sink, her brandy glass, her gauzy curtains. I began snipping straightaway.

Kitchen sink from *Velkom to Inklandt,* papercut (2017).

The papercuts I made for what became *Velkom to Inklandt* do not illustrate the poems, but run beside them, as portals to an ordinary twentieth-century domestic interior. They could belong to anybody's grandmother. That's why, instead of closing the poems into a singular experience, as per an early suggestion from the press, to draw Liesl, or a family tree, I hope instead they open it up to a general reader who, chances are, has also encountered a hair brush, a loaf of bread, a packet of fags.

Poems don't need illustration. Paintings don't need words. In fact image and text are often natural enemies. Yet, when they are allowed space to coexist, they can become unexpected allies. There are so many examples of this situation. Think of how the labels in galleries make you feel. Sometimes they seem essential, sometimes nauseating. The headline captions under photos in the news. Advertising and social media. Think of the billing on an illustrated book – the writer's name in big letters, the illustrator's name sometimes not even included! There is power and status conferred on writers (aaah, the wielders of language!) and often a kind of dismissal of illustration, as if it isn't doing much besides prettying up the pages. Maybe it isn't. (A lot of this is historically gendered: ladies' work, like embroidery, also an underrated area of great creative possibility.) In children's books, there is a lot more equality, e.g. Julia Donaldson and Axel Scheffler share the credit for creating the iconic *The Gruffalo*. But still, think of the status of a person writing for adults as opposed to someone who writes for small children! And how we are supposed to grow up and not need pictures any more! Surely it's because we miss pictures so much as adults, that cookery and gardening books do so well.

Example 2. The other way round: paintings spawn poems

A few months ago, I went to the opening do of a painting show at a small commercial gallery off Bond Street. The artist showing, Danny Markey, is a colleague of mine at the Royal Drawing School, one of the places I regularly teach. I really like his loose observational small-scale paintings, and, as I hardly knew anybody there to chat to, I decided to look at the work attentively and write. I wrote about eight poems, each riffing from a different small painting. I typed up and edited the poems when I got home, but kept the edits minimal, as I didn't want the words I'd scrawled to lose the liveliness and informality of my observations, which were a mirror to Danny's spontaneous and gestural paintwork. I emailed the poems to him. He was pleased, and asked if I could allow for their use in the gallery print out or the next catalogue. It all seemed a bit complicated to move it to a more official stage, and I haven't sent the poems out for publication either. In a way, it wasn't about whether the poems were 'good' or 'publishable', but about close looking and responding. Process not product! I was able to 'get inside' the brush marks and drift into the yellow, pink and red of the artist's painted world, just by the use of my eye and a nice ink pen, and 'right myself' in the middle of the traffic dense and ostentatiously materialistic centre of this city. I often do this if I'm at an exhibition by myself. It makes me engage with the work very differently, using my senses and my own creative powers rather than my critical eye. Poetry and painting become allies in this situation, creating a space free of consumerism and commerce, where the connection is sensory, questioning, bodily.

I am aware that earning a living is also crucial to maintaining one's artistic practices, and that I have been privileged to grow up a long time ago, when I had a grant to go to art school and tuition was free, when housing was (more) affordable and before benefits had been decimated. This gave me opportunities to live and develop my work on a very low budget. I know how arduous and dispiriting it can be to try and find a sustainable income as any type of artist. This is partly what has informed my endless collaborations and attempts to answer briefs, and compromise towards outcomes in favour of accessibility, so that the work can be enjoyed or reach out to as many people as possible. In the case of a book, if illustrations help to sell it, and one day I get royalty payments, then great.

When I teach on the subject of poetry to my art students, they are often intimidated, many not having looked at a poem since school, and being apprehensive in case intellectual rigour or analytical scrutiny are required. That's why I start with this (slightly embroidered) quotation from Octavio Paz.

I ask them to bathe in the poem (is its water hot or cold?), copy it out onto a scrap of paper and take it to the shops to use as an alternative groceries list, read it from bottom to top like a ladder up to the opening line, (above which sits the poet's knotty head), read it slowly out loud into their smart dumb phones voice memo facility and play it back.

These are ways to feel the weight, colour, texture, rhythm, composition and tone of the poem.

You can inhabit the poem like a well-cut suit, swaggering in the luxury of its velvet.

Or occupy the poem like a shingle beach, feel its stones in your toes. You can drift into the poem's apparently harmless flames, and find yourself eternally scarred by its burn!

It is a juicy thrill to set up an arrangement of images before a reader or viewer, and hope that the arrangement takes them, by a mysterious form of transport, into the world of their own experience or feeling. There is magic in recognising, with a heart-stopping thud, something one has never seen before, or something forgotten, or something only known secretly to the self, in a buried way. My approach to making things begins with instinct and observation, and aims for connection. My way of combining art forms is play led and I let the materials I'm using lead me towards what I'm hoping to find out about and talk about in the work. If there is need for an intellectual honing of the work, that comes in only at the end. It's rare for me to start with an idea. I rummage towards the unknown, taking with me my reader-mind, full of language, my painter's equipment: colours and brushes.

ACTIVITY: Poetry into collage / collage into poem

Go and get an anthology from the shelf or the library now. Open it at random. Read the poem you see. Read it again. Read it again. Is it a poem you have never read before? Great. By a poet you have never heard of? Wonderful.

Spend some time with the poem and explore it using those questions I touched on earlier: read it and look at it for texture, colour, tone, rhythm, composition, mood, register, weight, movement, voice ...

Is the poem yellow with streaks of mauve and black? Does it start heavy and end light, or the other way around? Maybe it's relentlessly light all the way through... What about the appearance of the poem? Does it hinge on its layout, use rhyme, a particular traditional form? Is there a lot of white space around it, between words? What happens in your body as you read it? Can your breath manage the line length sitting down, or is it better if you stand up? Does it make your heart sink, or your head explode, or does it elicit a little sigh, or a big laugh? Is it made of denim, gravy, revolution or starlings?

Get some colourful scraps of paper, some with patterns and textures, and make a collage, a non-verbal version of the poem, honouring the textures and colours you found by finding visual equivalents. This is difficult but fun, is a form of translation and certainly needn't be slavish or even faithful. If the poem you picked out contains a frog, you don't need to draw one. But make your collage do as much frog stuff as the poem does. This might mean giving it the essence of croak, or an amphibious leap from one material to the next, or using scale so that the person looking at the page can feel as small as a frog or as large as a person in relation to a frog. Maybe when it comes to art making you are a tadpole. But as Norman MacCaig said, "Throwing things away can be as enjoyable as making them", so have a recycling bin handy. Do this exercise over and over again – alone or with a friend or a group. One day you may find you've made enough collages that you find satisfying or interesting that you can use them to inspire a new sequence of poems.

In this exercise, there is a template for collaboration and expansion inherent. Poems can lead to collages which can lead to poems. This creative responding can inspire a lot more reading, risk taking in terms of taste, and an expanded enjoyment of looking, not only at art and poetry, but at the world.

Arji Manuelpillai

So, You Wanna Make a Podcast?

Nowadays everybody got a podcast! said a good friend of mine. That would have surprised a lot of people a decade ago. Back then, we thought it was all about visuals, 3D and high-intensity immersive experiences. But it turns out people want background voice, they want something while journeying to work, cooking or running. People want grassroots set-ups presented with honesty, authenticity and passion by people like them. Yes, there is a hell of a lot of corporate rubbish in the podcasting world but let me assure you, there is still space out there for your idea; your podcast is worth the effort, your podcast deserves to be made.

My name is Arji Manuelpillai. I'm the host, producer, writer, organiser, editor, sound engineer and marketing exec with *Arji's Poetry Pickle Jar*. It's a podcast you may or may not have heard of. I started it in those dark days of lockdown where every part of me was saying *Do something or you will destroy yourself!* So, on a laptop that sounded like it was perpetually taking off, with audio software that made a blip bop sound if it was too close to the radiator and a mic that buzzed like a cheap sex toy, I began. My podcast grew from nothing with about 50 quid in total. In this short and punchy essay, I'm going to give you the lowdown of how, why and for whom I made this thing, with the hope that you too can make your own podcast and harass your friends and family to subscribe.

So first the 'why?' Since making this podcast I have complained, moaned and slammed the laptop more times than I can count. It is a labour of love, never funded, never supported by anyone, and yet, every month I receive 20+ emails from all across the world asking to be a part of it. Everybody wants to know the guy who makes the podcast! So the first reason is just pure ego. Rest assured there are ways to make money from the medium. Advertisements, sponsorships, subscriptions and perhaps arts funding are possible avenues. However, for me, it was always about the learning. When I started the podcast I wanted to improve my critical appreciation. I felt there was a gap in the market as everybody was obsessed with writing and I wanted to celebrate the act of reading. I wanted to use my audio skills and improve my speaking and improvising. I also found that people struggle with critiquing work: often reviews were hard to follow, involving long words and gravitas. I wanted conversations about poems that felt like they were happening in a pub. I say all this because if you are going to spend hours and hours creating a podcast, make sure it is adding to your personal creative goal as an artist and professional.

Last week, I was on a call with Liz Berry talking about horses. I mean, who doesn't want to talk to Liz Berry about horses. I don't have a masters or a PhD, but the podcast gave me an avenue to connect with poets whom I love and respect. A podcast is a business card. It has opened doors to events, it has allowed me to give talks here and abroad and it has also helped sell my book. At essence, I believe wholeheartedly that I am an important part of the British poetry scene. I wouldn't have come to that conclusion with just the release of my book.

So let's take a step back. The first and most important questions are: what is your idea? and who is it for? When you're creating a podcast the listener always has to be at the centre of the experience. How old is your target audience? When will they listen? How will they engage? What amount of time is perfect for that specific audience member? What ways do they get their information? These questions are central to your podcast because if you don't know your audience you will struggle to pitch your content. For example, if your podcast is for children but you are using vocabulary from the Middle Ages it just isn't going to fly.

So draw an image of your target audience member and label it with as many details as you can think of. What do they eat? What do they listen to? This will give you the opportunity to listen to a range of other podcasts in your field. Listen carefully. What are the things you like and dislike? What could you do better?

As much as figuring out and even drawing your target audience is important, remember that all these details can change. You may love the jingle as you come into a show but the statistics might show you lost 60 percent of your audience there. Test and learn, test and learn: it is key to your progress.

So now you have your target audience and you have your idea, let's get down to the structure. Audiences often like to know what they are getting. This means that in each episode I tend to focus that first three minutes making sure the audience understands what will occur. If it was an episode of 24, it'd be the voice that says *"Last week on 24 …"* Time is precious. Break down your podcast episodes into chunks of interaction. Write it up and edit it as you go along. You need to know exactly what you are doing before contacting guests or pressing record.

Within my podcast I work with this basic breakdown:
1. Introduce podcast and guest
2. Speak to guest about upcoming books or releases
3. Guest reads poem they love
4. Discuss poem together
5. I read chosen poem for the second time

I decided on how long each section would be and I then had a breakdown for the perfect episode. This created a blueprint for my podcast. Within this blueprint I added beds (background music), jingles (the bit that tells you the name of the show) and adverts (that's me telling you to subscribe).

I am a big believer in scripting sections and then letting free-flow conversation occur when it needs to. You don't have to be a linguistic whizz-kid, you just need an ability to write a decent paragraph. The best podcasts feel easy and unrehearsed, but the best podcasts are practised and rehearsed. Practise your delivery. Practise on your phone's Voice Memos. Yes, your friends will think you are weird, that is all part of it. Yes, you'll cringe when you hear how nasally your voice is – yes, it is scary! But don't give up. Listen close to your vocal ticks: the eeerrrrrrrs and aaaaahhhs, the tapping of a table leg. The more you practise, the better your recordings.

Next up, is learning how to record your podcast. There is a whole lot of cheap recording software out there. Probably most notable is Garageband as it is so easy to use. But there are also more expensive options like Ableton, Cubase and Logic Pro. Before working on this podcast, I had a history of audio editing. I've worked in studios, rapped, produced and played instruments. I started a youth radio station in Barnet, ran a radio station with young migrants and have even created one-off episodes for private clients. I use Logic Pro. I have a Focusrite external sound card and a Rode Mic. I record interviews through Zoom and I upload with the brilliant user-friendly online interface Anchor. If you bought my exact kit it would cost you about £400 (without the laptop). But I only invested in this tech on the fourth season of the show following a lucrative recording job. It's important to realise that podcast audiences deserve good quality but that the need for full-size, high-spec studios is no more. I spend time listening to podcasts that have truly awful audio but I put up with it for the interviews or the idea. If you do not have any editing software perhaps experiment with online editing software. Spotify for Podcasters is a great tool launched by Spotify earlier this year. Alternatively, it is also possible to record direct on the phone and audio edit in Garageband or Inshot. There are soooo many ways to skin this cat and there are a whole host of YouTube videos to help you do it.

Phew, we are finally through the technology jargon. I know, it was dull as hell but you're still here. After the recording process, you will be full of beans. Excited and enthusiastic. You want to share it! But now, unfortunately, the edit begins. Editing podcasts is very similar to editing poems. Long, frustrating and tiring. I remember Rishi Dastidar saying, "Write with fire in your veins, edit with ice." That's exactly the same with your podcast editing. You've got to murder your darlings. You've got to cut, slice, shift and split. Remember, your listeners are gold. Their time is precious. When I listen to a podcast, I want every single second to be useful. Be brutal in your editing and the fanbase will respond to that level of care.

But wait, there is a caveat to that. Don't edit for the rest of your life! Set a time period for the edit. Stick to it. I have met a whole lot of radio producers who started their podcast nine years ago and are still searching for that brilliant vocal take, that perfect guest, that seagull to be cut at 9.43. Everybody can edit but not everybody can finish a project they started. Getting to the finishing line means you have to do the best you can with the time and materials you have.

Before putting your podcast out there, it is important to do your snooping. That isn't a reference to Snoop Dogg, it's a term some radio people use when they listen back to a recording. Sit down with a cup of tea or take a long walk in the wilderness and have a close listen to your podcast. What works well? What sounds boring? At what points does it need to change? I am not expecting you to go back into the podcast and edit, no, snooping is about learning, growing and improving for future episodes.

After you have recorded your podcast, it is important to find a way to get it out there. A good marketing strategy isn't developed overnight. It requires finding a platform you enjoy and using it to promote your brand and your idea. Don't worry about doing everything badly, do the small things but make them count.

Remember, you have your target audience so pick social media that the target audience responds to. Create a folder of clips and images and drop them weekly. That could be a photograph of you setting a studio up, it could be a guest speaker's image, an audio clip from the show or a person's reaction quote. Build a folder of promotional hype. Mail your fans, your friends, your Mum and Dad, spread the promotion out over a longer sustained period. You don't want the fire to burn out too quickly.

And finally, you've done it. There isn't a fanfare or a fireworks display. BBC radio have yet to ring me up. But the feeling of being able to share a podcast is a beautiful thing. It's something to take pride in, something that is always online reminding people of the array of skills you've honed over the years. Take a moment to celebrate that first episode. It doesn't matter how many people listen, it only matters that you too have added to the world of podcasting and you too are further evidence that my mate was right: *nowadays everybody got a podcast.*

ACTIVITY

You may or may not want to make a podcast. However, I want you to imagine you are making a podcast just for five minutes.

- Explain your podcast in three minutes.
- Now, explain it in two minutes.
- Now explain it in one minute.
- Now explain it in ten words.

You could do the same exercise to explain your creative practice. It's a great way of pinpointing what you are good at, cutting away the small talk, the errs and uncertainties, and going straight to the gold.

Practice this pitch at home. Then go out into the real world and wow people with your self-knowledge and confidence!

Tamar Yoseloff

Innovation and Intervention:
Making Poetry Pamphlets

It was never my intention to start a press to produce poetry pamphlets, but, as things often go in the creative life, it happened out of accident and necessity. My route into publishing demonstrates that if you have a good idea which is outside of the prevailing trends in contemporary poetry publishing, sometimes it's better to do it yourself.

In 2011, I embarked on a collaboration with my friend, Vici MacDonald. Vici had been taking photographs of London's urban ruins – landscapes in which we shared a mutual interest – and I offered to write accompanying poems. As I trawled through hundreds of her photos, selecting ones that spoke to me, I chose to respond in sonnets – elegies to those worked-out and abandoned locations. After I'd written 14 poems to go with 14 photographs, I suggested to Vici that we might have the makings of a small book. It's worth mentioning that the publishing landscape has changed greatly in the subsequent years (more on that later), but, at the time, we had difficulty sparking interest. The poetry publishers we approached were uncertain how to market a 'hybrid' book. But as a graphic designer, Vici had very clear ideas about its visual appearance, and so we eventually decided to set up our own imprint and publish it independently.

First, we had to work out what to call our imprint. Vici lived on Hercules Road in Lambeth, near the site where William Blake made his first letter press publications, so we named ourselves 'Hercules Editions'. A grandiose name for a tiny project. But something of Blake's independent spirit chimed with what we were doing, so it was apposite, especially given our eventual direction.

We then set about educating ourselves in book production. Vici was used to instructing printers, and I had done some book layout in my time, so we weren't complete novices. As we wanted to be able to sell in bookshops, we had to purchase an ISBN – we discovered you could only buy them in tens, so we joked about what to do with the other nine! Then we located a company in Hackney who had a Risograph. We liked the grainy quality of Riso printing, which suited Vici's black and white photos and the sonorous tone of my poems.

We printed 300 of the first edition, and signed and numbered them – we wanted to present it like an art publication. We launched the book at the Poetry Café, to coincide with an exhibition of the photographs held there. That was followed a few months later by a second, expanded exhibition at the Poetry Library, which included 'objects' found at each of the featured sites. And then the unexpected happened – our little project was shortlisted for the Ted Hughes Prize for New Work in Poetry, an award that praised its hybrid blending of photographs and poems, the very thing that had made it difficult to place initially. We had never imagined it would inspire people in the way it did, as it was such a personal, and we believed, 'niche' project.

It was only after our shortlisting that we realised there was a gap in the market for making books that brought poetry and image together. Having already found a name, and with nine more ISBNs in hand, we launched our press.

We didn't know when we started that it would be a golden age for the poetry pamphlet. At events such as Free Verse Poetry Book Fair and the Small Publishers Fair we found kindred spirits – presses that were innovating the concept of the pamphlet (or 'chapbook', as we like to call it), such as Corbel Stone, Guillemot, Sidekick, Green Bottle, the Emma Press, Bad Betty and many more. These smaller publishers highlight the production values, typography, and illustrative elements of their books, to make the words they are promoting even more vital. It's no accident that these independent presses seemed to come at a moment when larger presses were failing, or no longer able to support the publication of new poetry due to greater commercial interests. Even in these times of recession, the production of the poetry pamphlet continues to thrive, because they are generally easier (and cheaper) to make. And sometimes, it's just better to do your own thing.

So twelve years into this unexpected life as a publisher, these are my thoughts about the poetry pamphlet and how to evolve a press:

1. What's the big idea? The ethos of Hercules Editions as it developed was to find a visual world for the poem projects we accepted. We never thought of this as illustration, rather a way of creating a landscape for the poems to live. The projects developed organically with the authors; sometimes we commissioned artists to work alongside our authors, we even commissioned authors to create their own visual responses. And we have retained that ethos ever since.

What sort of books do you want to create? What kind of poetry do you want to champion? Is there a gap in the market that you can fill? We ended up writing a manifesto, at first as a document to present to potential funders, but we found it was useful in reminding us of our purpose and goals. The excellent Broken Sleep Books champion working class and experimental poetry, and are committed to community engagement, offering one free subscription to their publications to a different low-income writer every month. Out-Spoken Press provide a platform for voices under-represented in mainstream publishing and hosts an emerging poets development scheme. Hazel Press produces books that are informed with the environment and climate crisis. Their publications are printed on recycled paper using vegetable-based inks to keep their printing methods as environmentally friendly as possible. What could your new offer add to the mix?

2. Funding. As I've just mentioned funding, it's important to consider how you will finance your press. We have been fortunate over the years to get project grants from Arts Council England, but you need to be ready to navigate their application process, which is lengthy and detailed. They will expect you to have all your costs and timings in place, and to meet particular criteria. If you feel uncertain about tackling all that, there are smaller funding bodies and borough councils who may be willing to back you (particularly if there are local interests involved). We have also relied on crowdfunding, which is an excellent way of raising money, particularly if you can give your donors something of value or a way of being directly involved with the book or with the author. We always offer our donors an opportunity to have their names in our books, and we hold special workshops and one-to-one tutorials with our authors for our most generous supporters.

3. Distribution and sales. Vici and I always ran the press out of our homes. Our print runs and the books themselves were small enough to store, and we have always handled our own dispatch. You can find companies who will handle distribution and storage for a percentage. Many smaller UK presses use Inpress (inpressbooks.co.uk) for their distribution, particularly if you want to be stocked in bookshops, but if your output is small, it might be best to do this yourself.

Hercules publications are available in a small number of bookshops, but the bulk of sales are made through our website (we accept PayPal, which we find is the easiest and least expensive platform for payments). We also sell at some of the smaller book fairs and live events. For these, we have invested in a card reader, which is simple to use and makes it possible to take cashless payment.

4. Printing. Hercules books are digitally printed by a commercial firm. We shopped around until we located our current printer with whom we've developed a good working relationship. But with the cost of printing and paper going up, we are also considering print on demand, which makes it possible to do smaller runs – a good option if you don't have a lot of cash up front.

Depending on how your books are going to be produced, you might want to invest in the equipment to print yourself. Presses such as Paekakariki and Clayhanger use letterpress printers and their books are made in-house. You may want to do everything by hand – artists such as Nancy Campbell and Sophie Herxheimer have made their own publications (and often teach workshops on how to do it yourself) but have also worked with print studios and independent publishers in a more collaborative way.

5. Marketing. This is an age of accessible social media, so you can get the word out easily and without spending money on additional advertising. It's also simple to create a website for your press. Hercules have developed a mailing list with a thousand subscribers, and we send out a seasonal newsletter to people who sign up through our site.

We have always organised in-person launches for all our books, and have sought unique venues, particularly as many of our publications have a site-specific element. We try to work collaboratively with organisations; we pitched an event with Hannah Lowe exploring the Chinese community in Limehouse to the Museum of London Docklands, who were happy to promote and host the talk. We started featuring Zoom launches during lockdown and continue Zoom events occasionally – we can have up to 3-4 times the number of attendees at Zoom launches, which are much cheaper to run (although you do tend to sell more books at live events).

6. Innovation. Vici and I knew from the start how we wanted our books to look. We came up with a small square format for

Formerly, to reflect both photographs and sonnets. The shape was easily recognisable and distinct from other publishers, so we decided to retain it for future publications. People often comment on how portable our books are, how you can carry them in a pocket.

Vici created a striking colophon logo: a capital **H** with a lower-case **e** as its cross bar. We had badges made with our logo, which we continue to give out to our authors and readers – yet another way of promoting recognition.

Consider the personality of your press, and how you create a visual world that makes what you do distinct and memorable.

But perhaps the most important element of starting a press is to publish what you believe in, what you love – whether it's your own work, or the work of other poets. The poetry community has always supported and nurtured new voices and new ways of bringing poetry to the public, so you already have a generous audience for whatever you want to make.

ACTIVITY: How to put together a pamphlet collection

Locate a poem or group of poems that you've been working on to develop as a sequence (you will want around 24 poems for a pamphlet).

How can you expand on what you've already written, either by theme or form or narrative (can more than one voice tell the same story)? I sometimes write a response to a poem by taking the last line and making it the first line of a new poem (often kicking away the first line once it's finished).

How might you add other elements such as illustrations, or prose interventions?

Jane Burn

Paint and Poems: The Aggregate Life

In a room full of people, someone will invariably ask: *what do you do?* Pigeonholing seems to grease our social wheels – this person is a farmer / politician / teacher / checkout operator / other, therefore I'm going to adore / avoid them like the plague. That person has / has not forged a similar path.

We can work out whether (or not) to stay or move swiftly on.

I prefer to remain purposefully oblique, replying with such statements as *oh, I've been doing a lot of gardening at the moment,* or *I really enjoy toast.* By doing this, we might have to look a little deeper. We might discover inspiring, valuable acquaintances safe from the preventative assumptions which could have kept us apart.

It's my way of saying, *like me as I am,* of refusing demarcation, slipping definition's noose. There are so many versions of me it seems wrong to have to choose.

Just pick something and stick to it, can't you? has often been aimed at me. As has *Jack of all trades* – if you research the saying's provenance, you'll discover it was used, apparently, to describe William Shakespeare;

> … a playwright who was always … help[ing] with the stage, the set and the costumes. He would remember lines and try directing.
>
> (Cook, J. 2021)

Do you think those ingredients made him more aware of a play's successful recipe? You can bet your bottom dollar they did. *Master of none,* tacked on later, morphed the saying into cautionary tale; one might possess scraps of knowledge, but lack real ability in anything. Je conteste cela![1]

I defy the neat package. I'd be easier to market, for sure, but I am content to slip through definition's sieve. I am working class, autistic, pansexual – a mother, friend, partner. A writer and an artist.

Dissecting further, I'm not exclusively an eco, nature, confessional / other poet, not exclusively a painter, printmaker, illustrator, textile artist / other executant.

I've already lived many creative lives. How could I cling to one discipline, when there are so many to be interested in? I'm hybrid, in art and making, hybrid in writing, **hybrid in everything**.

How might hybridity inform poetic practice? Plutarch's *Moralia* attributes a most pertinent saying to Ancient Greek poet Simonides:

> ... Simonides calls painting silent poetry, and poetry speaking painting ... what the one sets forth in colours and figures, the other relates in words and sentences ...
>
> (Plutarch 10th/13th Centuries/1874)

Poetry and art are close kin, encompassing individual interpretations of emotion, nature, place, science, history, faith, mythology, item or experience. Both are thought made manifest. My mixed-media piece *Siren* serves as an example of the journey from internal research to external life. She's descended from mythology, adapted to fit my mind, then born of me. One day, this picture will help translate her story into text. As a painting or poem, she's alive inside my head.

---

1. I dispute this.

Figure 1: Siren

Poetry is a nourisher of art; take Millais's *Ophelia* (1851), Cy Twombly's *Hero and Leander* (1985), and Dina El Sioufi's *Double Entendre* (2020), to name a few. Art returns the favour, bestowing upon poets the infinitely exciting gift of ekphrasis. The Latin phrase *ut pictura poesis* (uut pik-too-ră poh-ees-is) translates to ***as painting is, so is poetry***. It was used by Horace in his *Ars Poetica*, 19 BC.

> "Poets and painters, though, have always shared / The right of trying
> anything they dared–"
>
> (Horace, 19 BC/1953)

There is an artwork – *Ut Pictura Poesis* – by Charles-François Hutin (1745–1746) which adopts this phrase as its title. It's a busy scene –

> various figures clamour and create:
> sculpting tools, palettes, and brushes,
> books and trumpets liberally abound.
> You can imagine the hubbub in the hall.

It's a sensory nightmare. I couldn't create if I were there. This picture serves as a reminder not let my own practice descend into cacophony – tempting though it might be to juggle twelve projects at once, I have learned to keep no more than five at once in the air, otherwise I run the risk of ending up in Hutin's hall,

> shuddering in a corner,
> snapping paintbrushes
> in half, babbling scraps of verse.

Yes, there are incredible similarities between art and poetry. Both require an emptying of your head onto suitable receptacles. We're all trying to recreate something about the world around us, be it abstract or concrete. Try not to think about Plato: according to his character Socrates in *The Republic: Book X*, he would have banished the lot of us from his ideal because our works are

> … imitations thrice removed from the truth …
> (Sparknotes, n.d.)

Ouch. Well, Plato, you're right in that I cannot manufacture a living bird, tree or ocean. But I *can* tell the world, using whichever medium I choose at the time, what a bird, tree or ocean means to *me*. Those meanings are, in my opinion, real as DNA. Everything ingested by human senses is translated to suit that human's specific beliefs, preferences, requirements and personality. Everything is truth while we are telling it. It's all mimesis – even fiction sparks from or contains kernels of truth.

Truth is art because art is the beating heart of everything.

It seems painting and poetry were destined to live side by side.

No one art is more important than another. Art is egalitarian.

As artists, we discover, through trial, error and practice, which branch we prefer to roost upon. If you are anything like me, you find yourself excited by the whole tree, flitting from branch to absorbing, enjoyable, fascinating branch.

I'm a polymathic bird, a tripartite soul – my composites are art, craft and writing. I need them all if I'm to be my own utopia. Be complete.

Words and images negotiate this intoxicating inheritance between genres – think of parietal art; illuminated manuscripts, artists' books like Blake's *Songs of Innocence and of Experience* (1789) or *Танго с Коровами* (*Tango with Cows*) by Vasily Kamensky (1914). The indeterminacy of the Fluxus community (1930s-1970s). Filmpoems. We're custodians, carrying this amazing heritage forward, adding breakthroughs of our own along the way.

In concretism, for example, we have the sense
neither image nor poetry is enough alone –
to satisfy their creator, they must combine.

> We must be prepared to contemplate poems as constellations of words, as ideograms, as word pictures, as permutational systems.
> (Solt, 1985)

In photopoetry, found and collage (like Anne Carson's *Insomnia Dog*, 2022), we find symbiosis, a collaborative colloquy between oscillating versions of reality.

> [We discover]… the visual immediacy of the … image against the unravelling, modifying, accumulating verbal images that emerge from the poem … visual and verbal images blend, clash, contradict, embolden, evoke and resist … encourage the 'obliquity' and 'serendipity' of text and image.
> (Nott, M. 2018, p.4)

Here, overleaf, are examples of my own found / poemcollage, and of my picturepoems, which I'll also explore next:

Figure 2: Who's Who

Figure 3: The Open-palmed Man

Figure 4: Words Sung in Shapes of Light. After the Baptistery Window, by John Piper, Coventry Cathedral.

Figure 5: Sonnet / When You and I Were Sky and Tide

Figure 6: Blue Land

Figure 7: A Garden's Year Begins

I also create picturepoems. An image can sometimes prove too strong to be denied, unwilling to be bound to the page by words alone. As I 'wrote' the experimental poems on the previous page, I found expression via text alone insufficient in conveying powerful senses of colour and light. I needed to taste colour, fill the lines with colour.

Colour wished to speak for itself.

It felt rebellious and thrilling to allow it to do so, denying traditional urges to bind a poem within textual representation. The visuals claim the body of the poem.

Text and image synthesise.

Picturepoems can assist a poem's formation, unriddle intentions and shape. Sometimes, poems ask to go beyond picturepoem and wear the guise of words. Take, for instance, *Sonnet / When You and I Were Sky and Tide* – painting this version tells me that, should the poem remake textually, it must contain

ebb,

flow,

mirroring –

a sense

of distance

and light.

Asemic writing is another vital part of my practice. There is freedom in this curious distribution of text-yet-not-text, this

> ... wordless, open semantic form of writing ... a shadow, impression, and abstraction of conventional writing. It uses the constraints of writerly gestures and the full developments of abstract art to divulge its main purpose: total freedom beyond literary expression.
>
> (Jacobson, M. n.d.)

It's a means of reconciling surrounding sensory data, of testing possible landscapes for a body of work. In my asemic poem *A Garden's Year Begins* (Figure: 7), everything began as tones of soil, finger smudges of beloved dirt, emerging colours of growth, before enmeshing with the emotional terrain that I, as an autistic person, negotiate while spending time there.

I count this essay as an example of art informing words. One of the reasons I adore the hybrid / lyric essay is its layout upon the page. It's not just reading words that gets me excited. I can examine and respond to a text's recto / verso habitation, its action / reaction amongst white space. When I'm building a collection of my own, I find it helpful to screenshot page selections and assess its optic-to-text parlance; to take an aerial view of the paper acres. There is more to a poem than words.

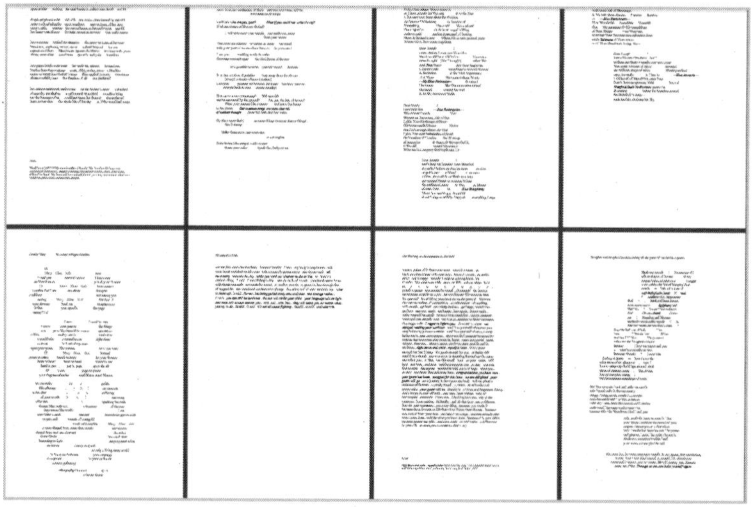

Figure 8: Poem/Page Screenshot

I have often questioned polymathy. Is it beneficial or detrimental to practice? What would life be like without this multivalent drive? If I had settled upon certainty, would it be clearer where I wished to be?

I would maybe be a better fit for more circles and circumstances.

I could direct my focus absolutely toward one thing.

I could write a PhD proposal, for example, which pursues one thread, rather than baffle institutions with an application which gallops after twelve, swerves leftfield, diverts onto another route, goes round the houses and

falls

from

a

cliff –

one that would take twenty years to complete, and not three.

I used to worry I was doing nothing to the best of my ability (*master of none*, remember?). It is possible to find rapture in too many things? Of course, one must sometimes exist within a particular enclave for a while – there are jobs we must do for a living, deadlines to meet, current creative obsessions to slake. When one art takes precedence for too long, however, another part of me suffers. I'm aggregate. When one craft becomes all-consuming, my axis tilts; the first increments of unbalance pass unnoticed, but just as the centimetre out at one end becomes the metre out at the other, I am doomed to destabilise.

Poetry is an outlet for my mind's extremities –
pinnacles and slumps, rage and obsession,
memories foul and fair.
Poems are documentations upon life's blade.
Poems always, in some way, accommodate pain.

Painting / drawing / sculpture is an outlet for beauty, pleasure, euphoria, detail, texture; the handling of tools, strokes with a brush. Hyperfocus encourages the exclusion of outside interference. I become entirely distanced from the stress of text-based interaction. I lose myself in the expanse of the outside world. I'm happy, for a while, to vanish into the enthrallment of each pigment.

Figure 9: Found (the foundation upon which my poem The National Trust Cannot Charge You to Come In[2] *was built)*

Sewing and crafting are outlets which nourish through detailed repetitiveness, triggering subconscious contemplation and fostering a state of comfortable numbness[3].

These actions for me are akin to stimming – here I find the purest form of recovery. In these moments, I stitch myself into a blissful blank, and after my mind has taken the time it needs to rest and reset, I arrive at a place where thoughts and ideas thrive – thoughts and ideas I usually didn't know I needed to have.

Using gentle self-interrogation, I have fathomed some of the reasons I do what I do.

---

2. This poem was first published in *Poetry London*
3. Borrowed from *Comfortably Numb*, Pink Floyd,written by David Jon Gilmour and Roger Waters.

Creativity has given me the courage,
desire and capacity to communicate.
After forty years of giving in, giving up,
being side-lined, forgotten, bullied,
criticised and discounted –
after decades of shyness, shame, confusion and fear,
I found there was so much to say
it required numerous means to say it.

If I am to achieve polyphony of mind, heart and soul, I must match my needs to their appropriate means of expression. Each art I use extends and encourages my confidence, fluency and articulacy.

This is multi-strand creative nourishment.

I realised I *was* doing something to the best of my ability.

I was hybridising the heck out of life.

I did something I never thought possible. I found a voice, stood up to be counted.

I blossomed, became an artist and a writer. I mattered. Forgot to feel afraid.

I hope that there will always be a place for such idiosyncratic reinterpretations of form. If so, the future of poetry can only increase in reach, appeal, longevity; expand inclusivity and interpretation, be more diverse.

Go where art takes you. Love every artist that you are.

ACTIVITY: Sense and cypherability – shaping poetic symbols of your own

Asemic writing is a fascinating subject. It disrupts your comfort zone, which is often no bad thing. It can shake up dull routine and challenge your creative thinking, set you on previously unknown paths. It can reveal aspects of your poems that you may not have thought about. It offers ways into and through your ideas, especially if you are wrangling with one of those pieces of work that simply refuses to kickstart.

> The signs before our eyes don't belong to any familiar system ... they put themselves forward in the form of a sign system, recognizable as marks disposed on a page ... replacing the expected message with an unexpected focus on ... the markings on the page.
>
> (Schwenger, P. 2019, p.2)

I chose asemic writing as it is something that incorporates ideates of polymathy without requiring stockpiles of art materials, because not everyone has access to those. This exercise only requires paper and a pencil or pen. Of course, if you wish, use as many different mediums as you deem fit. Throw in colour and varied pen / brushstrokes if the mood strikes. Make your page as large or small as feels right.

To increase accessibility, instead of paper and pen, sound recordings could be used. Try making sounds that are not words, yet somehow represent a language of your own: an asemic soundscape which assembles into poetic life; beat out asemic rhythms. Try asemic sensoryscapes: how might touching or feeling 'speak' a piece of creative writing into being?

1). Think about several items or creature names. In my example below I chose:

| pinecone | carnation | dog | tree |
| swan | bumblebee | frog. | |

2). Repeat the names you have chosen numerous times and notice the rise and fall of sound, the behaviour of syllables, the feel of them in your mind or mouth, the behaviour of your lips and tongue. As the names feed though, imagine yourself as a vital signs monitor – the way the *blip - blip - blips* travel across the screen, the way they waver and disrupt upon the horizontal line.

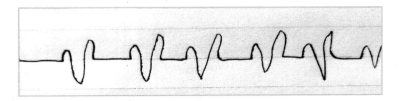

3). Have a go at representing the word's behaviour. I elected to use a page and a pen and scribbled down my written translations of each word-sound. What worked for me at the very beginning was placing the pen's nib near the line in readiness, closing my eyes, repeating the word a few times before allowing my subconscious to drive your asemic symbol for the word onto the page. I then repeated the symbol with my eyes open. You can see my attempts here:

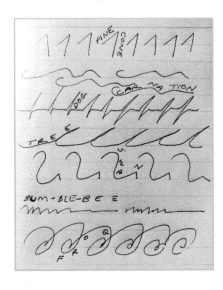

4). Choose one of your symbols. Spend time contemplating your item/creature. Think about what it triggers in your mind – this could be feelings, sights, sounds, concrete or abstract details. I chose to concentrate on 'swan' and developed mental pictures around it. I thought of:

water ripples   light   reflections   feathers
me, standing on the bank watching the swan

and made symbol for each of these:

5). Be brave and make a first draft of your asemic piece. Really let that subconscious fly! I found it helped to do this when I knew I was on my own – it's easy, at first, to feel uncomfortable, or a little embarrassed by these unfamiliar actions. Trust yourself. Make the marks it feels right to make. After all, nobody need witness the products of your experimentation, unless you wish them to. Trust me; your confidence will grow.

6). Has your first draft captured all/none/some of the elements as you imagined they would? This is the time to ask yourself such questions. If yes, great, If not, why? Your asemic brainstorm has hopefully clarified some ideas for you. When I examined mine (see above), I found it cluttered, frantic and not at all swan-like, yet it helped me to distil what I felt was important, which was these three components:

swan and reflections (pink circle)   me observing the
swan (green circle)   water (blue circle)

What the asemic brainstorm had settled in my mind was the
recollections I have of standing on riverbanks watching these
beautiful birds.

7). Take the vital elements of your piece and bring them together
on a fresh page. First, I filled the notebook's lines with a story of
water.

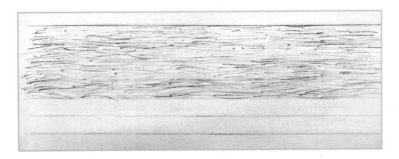

I added my swan symbol on the first line, as if it were a horizon.
I thought of myself standing on the bank (represented by the

last line), though in this version, the 'me' symbol does not, in the end, appear. My cast shadow and the swan's reflection are written into each other, in an unbroken line, as if somehow in that moment, we became one – "...allow[ing] the implications of the shapes on the page to evoke corresponding emotional gestures in the mind." (Schwenger, P. 2019, p.149)

8). Leave your asemic piece as it is or translate it onwards into text. Either way, I hope you enjoyed this prompt and wish you all the very best with your writing.

Works Cited:

Carson, Anne. *Insomnia Dog*. Three Fold Press, 2022. https://threefoldpress.org/annecarson Last accessed 13th April, 2023.

Cook, Jodie. 'Why Being A Jack Of All Trades Is Essential For Success', Forbes, 13th May, 2021. https://www.forbes.com/sites/jodiecook/2021/05/13/why-being-a-jack-of-all-trades-is-essential-for-success/ Last accessed 9th April, 2023

Horace (2005) *Ars Poetica Or Epistle To The Pisos* (sections AP: 1–37 On unity and harmony & AP:333-365 Combine instruction with pleasure). Translated by A. S. Kline. Poetry in Translation (Original work published 19 BC). https://www.poetryintranslation.com/PITBR/Latin/HoraceArsPoetica.php#anchor_Toc98156240. Last accessed 9th April, 2023.

Kamensky, V. (1914) *Tango with Cows*. Translated from the Russian by Daniel Mellis and Eugene Ostashevsky, 2022. https://tangowithcows.com/tango-s-korovami

Nott, Michael. *Photopoetry 1845–2015, a Critical History*. Bloomsbury Visual Arts, 2018.

Plutarch (1874), *De gloria Atheniensium* (section 3) Plutarch's Morals. Translated from the Greek by several hands. Corrected and revised by William W. Goodwin, PhD. Boston. Little, Brown, and Co. Cambridge. Press Of John Wilson and son. 1874 (Original work dates from 10th–13th centuries) http://data.perseus.org/citations/urn:cts:greekLit:tlg0007.tlg088.perseus-eng2:3 Last accessed 9th April, 2023.

Schwenger, Peter. *Asemic: The Art of Writing*. University of Minnesota Press, 2019.

Solt, Mary Ellen. *Words and Spaces*. Unpublished, 1985. https://writing.upenn.edu/epc/authors/solt/index.html Last accessed 12th April, 2023.

Plato, *The Republic: Book X*. Plato. Sparknotes, n.d. https://www.sparknotes.com/philosophy/republic/full-text/book-x/ Last accessed 9th April, 2023.

Ut Pictura Poesis. The Cleveland Museum of Art, n.d. https://www.clevelandart.org/art/1998.76

Helen Dewbery

Making a Poetry Film

For my first poetry film I used still images from a trip to New York. Using a basic editing program, I added a voiceover for the text, ambient noise of the bustling city streets, converted the images to black and white and added some movement across the screen. That was it: a simple poetry film aptly named *Arrival*.

Poetry film encompasses a variety of styles and genres, with filmmakers and animators working independently, poets working alone or collaborating with filmmakers, or production teams with large budgets. Each approach brings a different set of skills that impact the process and outcome. As a poetry film tutor and maker, I actively collaborate with poets to produce poetry films.

From the outset, I recognised that there is a combination of words, images, and sound that intrinsically creates a form of poetry itself. These pages will guide you in discovering this form for your poem, though they can be applied to other types of poetry film as well.

Choose the style and type of poetry film to suit the poem and what you want to achieve:

Poetic form	Animation
Abstract	Stop Motion
Conceptual	Dance
Location based	Personal essay
Archive	Performance
AI-generated	Ekphrastic
Music	Kinetic text
Lyric documentary	Split screen

or any combination of these.

Start with what you already know

The form of a poem is its physical structure and shape, and may involve its arrangement of sound and rhythms. In poetry film, structure comes from words and images – where frames and transitions can create enjambment, and the use of images, text and sound create rhythm and metre. Other poetic devices, such as repetition and metaphor, are also used. To this knowledge add basic visual language and film techniques. You don't need to become an expert, a general appreciation of the basics will go a long way.

What you need to make a poetry film:

1. Phone camera

I often use my phone camera to make a poetry film, and adding a video app and filters to the phone has given more creative options. To prevent black bars from appearing on the sides of my films I shoot in landscape mode which produces better looking videos (except when I want a vertical look, such as for split screen when I'm putting two or more images side by side).

There are two things that I always try and do: maintain a constant exposure across all my shots when filming, and transfer clips to my computer as soon as I can. The latter frees up space on my phone and keeps the clips more secure.

2. A poem

There are various options for the poem itself. The most popular choice is to use a poem that has already been written (perhaps use a poem you love that hasn't yet found a publisher). Alternatively, you can write a poem with the intention of using it for the film or create the text simultaneously with the images. You could also use a poem written by someone else or use just a section of a poem.

Both short and longer poems can work effectively. The important thing to consider is how you approach the poem. For instance, with a detailed poem, you can experiment with more abstracted imagery, whereas a poem with more space allows for more detailed visuals.

> 'They Are There But I Am Not' by Ye Mimi 葉覓覓影像詩作品 illustrates a series of moments to approach the concept of time. The pared down and whispered text works well with the detailed images.

3. Visuals

Start to gather video footage on your phone wherever you go. Additionally, you can use still photos already stored on your phone. I have a collection of images captured over several years that I often return to:

roads, pavements, transport, buildings, walls, fences, objects, doors, windows, wind, rain, sun, snow, walking, running, water, animals, landscape, fauna, trees, shadows, movement.

A store of images is a rich reservoir to dip into whenever you are searching for a shot. Archive or AI-generated visuals can also be explored and used.

> Ian Gibbins uses AI generated faces alongside actual people in 'The Life We Live is Not Life Itself' to explore life as a series of encounters and illusions.

4. Sound

When considering sound for your poetry film, think of it as a landscape (soundscape) with layers of immediate, mid-distance, and faraway sounds. Not all sounds require the same emphasis at any given time.

Your soundscape can include various elements such as:
- The spoken poem.
- Ambient or background sound. These are the sounds that make you feel like you are there: wind through trees, water, the hum of people or traffic.

- Sound effects like car tyres, a door closing, footsteps.
- Music.

Record sound separately from filming, rather than at the same time. This usually gives better results as you can concentrate on each task individually.

Although the sound recording capacity of phones has significantly improved, I can obtain higher quality sound by using a portable sound recorder. Get your hands on one if you can – it's the only piece of kit I would recommend investing in.

5. Video editing software

Search online for the most suitable video editing software that suits your budget, skill level, desired outcome, and whether you use a Mac or Android device. While some video editing apps are limited in scope, they are often user friendly and get the job done. Other apps offer more options and scope to experiment. All apps have online tutorials to help you get started and to get the best out of them. There are also apps and AI-powered tools that can be used to edit sound. Again, make an online search for the best one for you.

6. An idea

Every poetry film needs an idea. A referential or abstract trope that alludes to something beyond a literal interpretation of the poem. When planning a poetry film, I consider the poem's tone and mood, the intention of the poem, and whether I will subvert, juxtapose, or intensify it. I also think about any visual metaphors or symbolic meanings I can introduce. Sometimes I begin with a colour or sound, or I base the film in a specific location, perhaps where the poem is set or was written.

Once I have my idea, I create a written storyboard that includes all the elements of the poetry film, such as images, text, voiceover, music, transitions, and camera angles. This process is an essential aspect of my creative process and a valuable production tool.

A note on collaborating

If you are considering collaborating, my advice is to be an active collaborator with someone you know and trust. In some collaborations the poet may simply hand over their poem to the filmmaker. I prefer to work closely with the poet or musician, exchanging ideas and asking questions before the final poetry film is produced.

If you're interested in making poetry films yourself, forming a poetry film club with other poets is a great way to share ideas and skills – it's another form of collaboration.

'Making an Orchard' by Maeve O'Hair is about the making of an organic heritage orchard. There are also themes of loss, loneliness and single parenthood after the death of a spouse, and joy, love and leaving a legacy.

7. Visual language skills:

Visual language encompasses a range of techniques that can be used to direct the viewer's eye, enhance emotion, and add dramatic effect to a poetry film. Four key aspects to consider are colour, the rule of thirds, camera angles, and camera movement.

Colour: Colours have meaning. They can be used to convey mood and emotion or to create contrast and visual interest. Cool colours (think greens) bring a calming effect. Warm colours (think reds) tend to convey emotions ranging from happiness to violence. When placed alongside another, colours can appear harmonious, or they can have a much stronger visual impact.

As the narrative progresses in Be Manzini's 'This is Not a Thank You', the actors wear different colour t-shirts that correspond with passing time and changing emotions.

Rule of thirds: The rule of thirds is a compositional guideline that can create balance and interest in a shot. The frame is divided into thirds, using two horizontal and two vertical lines. The most important elements of the image are positioned at the intersection points. This makes the images visually captivating, and easy to read and comprehend.

Breaking the rule of thirds is useful too – it can add unease, disruption and alter power balance. Imagine a dog elegantly positioned on a third, then imagine that same dog large and imposing in the centre foreground of the screen, the camera looking up from below. A different story unfolds.

Camera angles and distance: Different camera angles can create a range of emotions, such as power or unease, intimacy or distance, and convey varying levels of information. For instance, the closer we get to a subject, the more we feel emotions like fear or sympathy. Shooting from above can make a subject appear smaller and vulnerable, while shooting from below can make it appear larger and more dominant. Additionally, being further away from a subject can convey a sense of distance or loneliness. The shot should be selected with purpose.

Movement: Camera movement, or movement within the shot, can suggest calmness and order or disruption, chaos and anxiety:

- Panning (moving the camera left to right or right to left) or tilting the camera up or down on a vertical axis, can reveal something, adding suspense and anticipation.
- Movement in the 'wrong' direction can add to unease.
- Something moving into the frame from the left feels more 'natural' than entering from the right.
- In *Woman Running Alone*, a film I made with Maria Taylor, a woman runs from left to right across the screen for the duration of the film – this creates a natural flow. Whereas if the runner was being chased, I may have changed the movement from right to left to add a sense of unease.

- I usually use a phone on a gimbal for filming, but sometimes I opt for handheld shots. Handheld shots can result in shaky footage that draws attention to the presence of the camera and the filmmaker, this can increase intensity or heighten tension. If shakiness is not relevant to the film's message, I keep the camera steady.

Like camera angles and distance, movement should be selected to enhance what you want to convey and be a conscious creative choice.

8. Editing Skills

During the editing process, I focus on how each shot transitions to the next, as well as the timing and duration of each shot. I may also use filters to modify the overall appearance of the film.

Transitions: I think of transitions to be like line breaks and punctuation. And the most commonly used transitions in poetry film are a straight cut and a dissolve.

The straight cut moves immediately from clip to clip. It represents a clear continuity in setting and time. It can be employed when creating repetition. The cuts can be in quick succession or more gently paced, depending on what effect is desired. In *Woman Running Alone*, I timed the straight cuts to match the cadence of the runner which in turn matched the rhythm of the poem and soundtrack.

A dissolve gradually transitions from one image to the next. The length of the transition is dictated by the mood or pacing of the film and poem. It can express emotion or time passing. For the duration that two images overlap, a third shot is created. In *Endlings*, a poetry film I made with Angela France, overlaps appear almost continuously to add to the sense of loss, memory, and hope that I saw in the poem. It's often in these third shots that magic appears.

> *Profile* by R. W. Perkins is a stream of consciousness with a montage of quickly changing still images that represent the sharing-every-moment of social media.

Filters: Most filters are designed to alter the colour and movement of clips. I use filters as a means of enhancing the overall aesthetic of the film. In *Woman Running Alone,* I applied a filter that converted every other image to mono, thereby toning down the overall colour effect and allowing for greater focus on the movement. Using filters thoughtfully and intentionally ensures that they serve a purpose rather than simply being used because they are there.

Editing the poem: The poem can also be edited as it finds its new form. When Kathy Gee was making *Fecund* she rewrote the poem several times for the film, changing the order and giving it an introduction and an ending. She also changed the rhythm slightly as she read the poem for the voice track.

> *Fecund* by Kathy Gee questions loneliness in response to hearing a quote on the radio.

A successful poetry film will be original and authentic, much like a poem on the page or a spoken poem. To achieve this:

- Avoid clichés and overly literal interpretations of the poem
- Incorporate a rich visual vocabulary.
- Make creative associations between the written, visual, and sound elements.
- Use a strong vocal delivery that heightens the metre and emotion of the poem, or create an imaginative use of text on screen.
- Have clear sound with no glitches.
- Leave space for the viewer.

A poetry film captures the energy and kinetics of the poem and utilises all available tools to convey it to the viewer. It doesn't leave the viewer questioning its purpose, wondering why they couldn't have just read the poem instead. By harnessing the power of the poem and translating it into a visual medium, a good poetry film creates a unique and engaging experience for the viewer where neither the words nor images would exist so satisfactorily without the other.

ACTVITY: Breath the poem in its location

When I'm creating a poetry film and the poem is specific to a place, I go there to breath the poem in its location. Even if a poem isn't about a physical location, I find a conceptual space. For instance, Lundy Island in the Bristol Channel became a portal to another world where I found shifting tectonics, maternal fractures and loss.

- Find a poem that is site specific or could occupy another real or conceptual space.
- If you can, go to the location and breath the poem – speak it out, breath it, close your eyes and sense it around you.
- Record the poem at the location if it's not too noisy (If it's windy, turn your back to the wind to shelter the phone's recorder).
- Record ambient / background sound at the location.
- Take film footage, or still images, using different camera angles and distance.
- Either at the location, or later at home, put the sounds and images together to make a poetry film.

Referenced poetry films:

Endlings, Helen Dewbery – https://vimeo.com/667960684

Woman Running Alone , Helen Dewbery – https://vimeo.com/494124463

Fecund, Kathy Gee – https://vimeo.com/383571935

The Life we Live is Not Life Itself, Ian Gibbins – https://poetryfilmlive.com/the-life-we-live-is-not-life-itself/

This is Not a Thank You, Be Manzini – https://www.youtube.com/watch?v=gl-yHih9D1w

They Are There But I Am Not, Ye Mimi 葉覓覓影像詩作品 –https://www.youtube.com/watch?v=2aF5l-YuFoU

Making an Orchard, Maeve O'Hair – https://vimeo.com/767827500

Profile, R. W. Perkins – https://www.youtube.com/watch?v=a3YA0s4Qx0E

They are there but I am not – https://vimeo.com/7695648

Caleb Parkin

Mycelia, Hedgerows and Tupperware: the Practical Sides of Wellbeing for Poets

A few years ago, I wrote a commission inspired by Bristol poet Thomas Chatterton, who died penniless in 1770 aged 18. His fame exponentially increased because of Henry Wallis' 1858 painting *The Death of Chatterton*. In it, a wan, redheaded Chatterton lies in his attic room, surrounded by scraps of drafts. He languishes on his unmade bed, purple breaches flopped waifishly to one side.

This, and similar images, have perpetuated the trope of the miserable, penniless poet. It's persistent and entrenched in popular imaginings of a 'professional poet' (an oxymoron in many people's mind). And while it might hold some louche and morbidly glamorous appeal – especially to the Victorian mind – there are alternatives. My experience has been that building up practical, entrepreneurial skills is key to our wellbeing as practising poets.

Poetry and wellbeing have always been entangled for me. Long before I thought about getting work published, I was writing for my own benefit – to figure things out, rant at the page and explore the persistent ideas and images which lingered in my mind. After I turned 30 and started to take poetry seriously, I began an MSc Creative Writing for Therapeutic Purposes, which offered theory to underpin a writing practice for its own sake, personally and with others. Now, those ideas underpin my workshops, even when they're not 'about' wellbeing. I'd like everyone to feel safe and able to express themselves, whatever happens with that draft after that session.

For some years, I felt frustrated and excluded by the practical aspects of being a poet: money, connections, knowledge, time –

and did I mention money? I know I'm not the only one. Despite growing up with parents who ran their own business, who were entrepreneurs, poetry never seemed a viable career. It remained a hobby, until such a time as I'd built up enough professional skills in other work – events, media production and education – to gradually move up and across, towards becoming a full-time poet (and now a full-time [funded] PhD student).

Many of us have experienced bad bosses – authoritarian, unreasonable, bullying even. It's possible, I believe, to flip that experience around and become the best possible bosses to ourselves: reflective, responsive and kind. I'm really passionate about sharing the practical skills around being a poet with those just starting to take it seriously as a vocation (which is how I see it), so we can be a community of good leaders, for ourselves and one another.

Wellbeing is, I think, practical. It's about considering our needs and taking steps to put those in place. It's about being assertive at times, to defend them. And it's about developing ways of working – which centre poetry and time to work on it – that work for you. I'd like to offer a few possibilities here which I've found helpful in keeping going, rather than expiring penniless on a chaise longue…

At the start of each section, I'll offer my own experience and what I learned from it, so you can perhaps be alert to and navigate a similar situation, before it happens. Often, I'll give a counterpoint experience too. I'll then offer practical ideas of how to act on each of these three main headings.

Your poetry mycelium
This section is adapted from a session I co-designed and -hosted with Nathalie Teitler, for the Poetry School. It was called 'Rooting Yourself' and, in it, we proposed creative and practical methods for exploring and consciously developing your networks. Some,

though not I, might call this (whisper it) *networking*. The verbing of that noun is unpopular because, I reckon, of a certain style of cynical, clambering networking which goes on. (And yes, I've met those 'networkers'!)

For me, a sense of connectedness and mutual support has been invaluable in keeping going and for my wellbeing. I'm part of critique groups, have co-chaired committees and am always open to new connections with like-minded poets and artists. We are, yes, a disparate bunch, but in my experience, there's a curiosity and wonder many poets share. And that means being in each other's company can be its own reward. Spontaneous moments of connection can also last: an ad hoc 1:1 lunch, or rowdy evening drinks, at a festival, for example.

It takes a while to find and develop your 'tribe' – those people you connect with in your approach to the work, and to the work around the work. It's possible you'll make some false starts, as I certainly have. On the flipside, you're likely to have moments where you'll find yourself in the company of poets you've looked up to and those who you'll come to know as your peers. Sharing those spaces, feeling able to say hello to those people next time you see them, is invaluable for our sense of connection and community.

Pause and think: for you, what is your 'poetry community'? Is it a microchip, a shoal of fish, a swarm of bees, or a nervous system? Are you a group of dancers, a pod of dolphins? Or does something else, perhaps gnarlier, come to mind: are you a pack of wolves (lovely as they are), a shoal of piranhas, a horde of zombies? Perhaps do some writing about this: what do these metaphors tell you and, where necessary, how might you transform your metaphor to one which feels more helpful?

There'll always be a sense of groups, I suspect – who's in, who's out, etc. I still have the odd moment of feeling I'm not in the 'right ones', to be honest. When that happens, I actively remind myself about my own Big Squishy Network, about the 1:1 relationships I have with poets and editors I've met over the years.

To consciously and genuinely build your own big squishy network(s) is a fundamental part of being a poet. These are relationships which can sustain and energise us, when poetry doesn't seem worth it – and they are relationships which could span decades. So why not invest in them, on purpose?

Some of the practical ways you might build your Big Squishy Networks (and which don't involve getting accepted on this or that programme):

- **Go on courses, get to festivals:** Local, online, wherever. (If money is tight, many organisations do reduced or free places.) I've met a lot of great people this way and stayed in touch with many of them, which might lead to …
- **Co-critiquing:** You've met poets on courses or approached them at open mic nights (another obvious one if you can). They seem at a similar point to you and you get each other. Why not ask if they'd like to try out swapping some poems? This could start as a few and build (as my networks have) to whole manuscripts. It's helpful to be clear about the kind of feedback you might want. There's a mutual accountability and trust here, which just costs one another's time.
- **Collectives:** If you're connected to a group of poets, perhaps you could become a collective? This might mean cheerleading for one another, sharing opportunities, commiserations, celebrations, having a coffee/pint sometimes. As ever, setting up some loose expectations about this – a manifesto or group alliance – is helpful to keep things convivial.
- **Critique groups:** If you're not in one of these yet, then set one up. Now we're all more aware of Zoom (or similar) there are options to work with poets pretty much anywhere. This takes some organising, but even having a session every other month, or whenever suits your co-conspirators.

- **Mentoring/being mentored:** Yes, these are often established through an organisation. But if you're working, would like to be mentored, and are prepared to invest some money in your poetry, could you approach someone directly? I've had good experiences of this, as both mentee and mentor.
- **Beyond poetry**... revel in your networks of Dungeons & Dragons players, Theremin-enthusiasts and whatever else you're into. Invite them to events, where you'll read poems inspired by your hockey matches. Having networks with artists, thinkers and doers beyond poetry is a Good Thing too.

Verdant boundaries

Earlier in my 'career', I was working with an organisation, hosting sessions for young people on a voluntary basis. The proviso was that once we'd developed the group and there was regular attendance, with a small waiting list, they would pay me a sessional rate. Once this criteria was fulfilled, I contacted the organisation about the sessional rate, as agreed. They said they had decided to use volunteers for all their arts-based work now, so were reneging on our agreement. A mentor said I should step away and seek collaborators who valued my expertise – so that's what I did.

It's hard to say No and to walk away from projects. But in my experience, moving towards relationships – especially with organisations – where your skills and art form are valued, will benefit you in the long-run. Sometimes, if I'm approached about something unpaid, and which seems evidently exploitative, I simply don't reply to the email. Agonising over that email is in itself unpaid labour and I'm not always prepared to do it! While it's a good thing to stand up for the rights of artists, when you feel resourced to do so, it's also not your job to do that work (on an organisation's behalf). Always consider what labour they're asking of you and step away when it becomes transparently extractive.

Pause and think: what do boundaries look, feel, sound, smell, taste like, for you? Are they made of brick, or steel? Are they more of a bubble, a mesh?

In her books *Emergent Strategy* (AK Press, 2017) and *Pleasure Activism* (AK Press, 2019), as well as on her blog (www.adriennemareebrown.net) writer and activist Adrienne Maree Brown often mentions boundaries. Instead of 'borders', we can think of boundaries as alive, active, organic – perhaps, Brown says, more like a hedgerow. Boundaries – including saying No – are the "container within which your yes is authentic". These boundaries can be verdant and vibrant, enabling activity elsewhere, safeguarding your writing time (or relaxing time).

Some practical measures to manage this:

Funding bids: If you're working with an organisation who are putting in a bid, be clear about what they need from you, when, and the proposed timescales. You might be corresponding with a salaried person whose relationship to the bid is different to yours as an artist (though a lot may also be at stake for them and the organisation). How can you give the right amount of input, at the right time – a biog, 200-word outline, a one-page description – rather than becoming entangled in the entire bid?

There's often a risk/reward ratio, but try to contribute the right amount of labour at the right time, rather than getting swept up. Where a new project or commission comes along, I'll be clear the first phone call and initial scoping chat is fine, then after that I am 'on the clock' and will anticipate payment for my time.

Plans B and C: If you invest a lot of time into a funding bid or application, consider your Plan B (and the Plan C for that). What you can do with that material if they say No – before you send it off. Have a backup plan, so that you know that work can be reused and recycled. It's important to feel the feelings of disappointment, have some moping time, and mourn the loss of that imagined future. Then, you can deploy your Plan Bs. You'll know when it's time to trash it all – but it's not on the first attempt.

Your 'agents': Putting yourself out there and hustling for work – however casually – can be exhausting. Not many poets have an agent – though there are some – because the sums involved wouldn't withstand their 10 or more %. However, there are people in organisations who can (and want to) act as an 'agent' of sorts for you.

Who might your 'agents' be in poetry organisations, or interdisciplinary fields? For me, this has been especially good for museums, interdisciplinary work, or in education. Intentionally developing your networks in various fields, not just poetry, can benefit your creative career and wellbeing. If people in – e.g. – your local museum service are chatting about engaging young people for an exhibition and you've done good work for them before, it's possible your name will come up.

Here are some things to consider in your relationships, with individuals and with organisations:

- What's the exchange? Sometimes we take on unpaid work because we care about the cause, or because we love the work and are in a position to take it on.
- If it's not paid, then question that exchange. For example, will the organisation be offering testimonials from participants, or some other in-kind support? Get this in writing, in a contract, Partnership Agreement, or similar.
- (Also, if you're taking on work unpaid, are you taking that work away from someone who is not able to take on unpaid work? It's been said before, but always bears repeating!)
- Talk money early. If they've approached you, does the organisation mention money in the first communication?
- If not, then that's an alarm bell to me and suggests it hasn't been considered. Don't be afraid to ask about money early

on. If they're not mentioning it, right away, it suggests a potentially rocky path ahead re: negotiation and payment.

- Being clear about boundaries at the earliest stages of collaboration can stave off a lot of potentially difficult negotiation later on. By articulating and making expectations explicit from the outset, we can avoid disappointment when they seem not to have been met later on.

Quantum Tupperware

The previous sections were about relationships with others, but this one is about your own relationship, to your work and to time. It's about getting things done, in a way which feels nourishing, kind to yourself, and not rooted in 'toxic productivity'.

In a previous role in TV programme production, I was at one point researching a slate of short inserts for a magazine-style programme (*The One Show*). It was a lot of work! But I really flew with it: moving between the different subjects, managing the different stages from development to contacting contributors, to setting up shoots.

Generally, working in organisations didn't go well for me: having to do things their way, navigating bureaucracies and office politics. I enjoy doing lots of things at once and am a little prone to distraction. I can achieve a great deal, just not always in the obvious, linear ways managers might expect. As such, moving into freelance life and PhD studies has suited me pretty well.

In his book *Messy: How to Be Creative and Resilient in a Tidy-Minded World*, Tim Harford makes the case for a 'network of enterprises': parallel projects, at different stages of completion, which 'cross-fertilise' one another, thus retaining their collective freshness in our attention. Inevitably, this can become – or feel – a little unruly at times (back to hedgerow images). But generally, this keeps my flitty mind engaged, gives processing time between and across projects, and allows for problem-solving on an unconscious basis, rather than stewing over something directly for too long.

However, and it's a large however, there were times earlier in my 'portfolio' working when it felt more like a trunk full of rocks. This was often when I'd taken on too much for too little – i.e. insufficient pay for the labour involved – and had at least one or more projects on the go which were a handbrake-turn-pivot from the others. Changing focus and direction, where a project doesn't fit in your network of enterprises, takes a lot of energy. As in, physical, brain energy – actual calories! (There is science on this.)

This has led to burnout, coupled with an earlier inability to articulate what was happening and what I needed. Not having a boss means you have to figure out what is going on yourself, with friends, partner, poet networks – and try to act on what you learn. It's more of a series of cycles than linear progression (see *Emergent Strategy* for more on this). I still have to make myself create pockets of time to stop, reflect, unpack what's going on – and it's never time wasted.

However you manage your poetry/writing/project capacity – around a full- or part-time job, or as a full-time freelancer – I've found that developing time management approaches which work for me has been crucial for my wellbeing. This means getting things done – not in a way which feels oppressive or laborious – so that you clear space for reading, writing, faffing about, playing in the garden, watching sci-fi, and being human. Here is what I've found works:

- **Plan fun stuff first.** What are you going to do this week that you'll really enjoy, on its own terms? I go dancing fortnightly on a Monday night and this is a fixed calendar date. Likewise, I book a couple of socials a week (in person or Zoom). This is vital, not additional. It makes the time I am working more focused and special too.
- **Consider your 'network of enterprises':** Whatever else you're doing – as a parent, carer, waiter, nurse, garden centre employee – does it inspire your writing in some way? If not,

is there a way you could rejig this area of your life so that it aligns with your network? (I realise this isn't always feasible, but is worth exploring consciously to see where changes might be possible.)

- **Old school diary:** I'm a visual thinker and remember by writing (unsurprisingly). So I use a diary with a week to view (Action Day, which I swear by), with tasks list to one side. (Yes, I also use computers, a lot – but a tangible, paper diary is ultimately how I stay organised.)
- **Boxes:** My diary has different boxes for general tasks, poetry-specific tasks (subs, editing, etc.) and one set aside for money, so I know what invoices I need to send that week. This has really helped me manage money anxieties, because I can see the income that is due (and, until fully-automated luxury queer space communism – that's important).
- I use the **bullet journal symbols** for what I've done, what's important, and what I'm parking for next week. Look them up: they're useful, and you don't have to use the whole system!
- **Project mindmap:** When I feel overwhelmed or the little-tidal-wave-of-anxiety is following me around, I mindmap all my projects: what, when, and the money each is bringing in. Seeing it all on one page is helpful (anxiety is often fuelled by a sense of the unknown) and this makes it more tangible. It's always 15 minutes well spent.
- **Straggler:** Based on this, can you see if there's something which is unrelated or doesn't feed into your other projects? Can you phase it out, or start thinking about changing it? What would the first stage of that be?
- **Start it:** You don't need to finish something in one sitting. I don't work well under deadline pressure. So when something is due a way off, I'll get it started – just a document with initial thoughts, fragments, a vague outline while I have it in mind. This might only take 10-20 minutes, but getting it started, having that initial splurge of ideas, means I can return to it, do a bit more, and that again it becomes less abstract.

- **Quantum Tupperware:** To keep something moving, I'll set aside some quantum Tupperware. This is especially important for poetry writing time. Do you really need a whole day, necessarily, to write poems? Or to go on a week-long retreat (though these are lovely, they're not accessible very often)? And is this, sometimes, an avoidance strategy? What time can you make in your day? Can you find 15 minutes? Having a more regular, briefer, writing practice could sustain your connection to it and keep the creative channels open. Trying to carve out whole days, or even hours, might be self-defeating. And, if you're like me, you can't always concentrate for that long anyway!
- **Realistic and adaptable goals, or 'chunking and chipping':** Instead of 'Write the essay for the Nine Arches Press handbook', I'll set the goal: 'Write the first heading…' (reader, I did). This suits my attention span and means I chunk down and chip away at several things in a week. I don't plan down to the minute or even the hour, instead leaving some flex for how I'm feeling that day.

A quote attributed to enigmatic poster boy for Bristol creativity, Banksy: "If you get tired, learn to rest, not to quit." Developing ways to make space in our creative lives for connection, play, exploration and – yes – rest is one of the ways we can keep going. I hope you found one or two useful tools in this chapter to fuel you and perhaps make a change or two which creates more space for your poetry to thrive.

Perhaps this wasn't what you were expecting for an essay about 'wellbeing' and poetry. But wellbeing isn't woolly or abstract: it's about identifying and addressing our needs. As practising poets, I think we need to consider the ground on which we're standing, making it solid enough to keep taking the risks poetry requires.

ACTIVITY

1. Being 'famous': Being an active member of the poetry 'community' isn't about becoming rich or renowned (though these are possible for a few!) – but about taking part, contributing, being a part of the dance.

Look up Naomi Shihab Nye's poem 'Famous' (it's variously online) and write your own version. For whom and for what would you like to be 'famous'? It doesn't mean being a celebrity. It's more about being a valued, generous presence to those who matter, to you.

2. Map your mycelium: If you'd like to extend this, then you could draw a map of your networks:

- On a piece of paper, draw yourself or a symbol for yourself.
- Around this, draw pictures, symbols, diagrams or words representing all the things, people and spaces that support your creative life (and you, theirs).
- Represent the nature of your connection to these supports:
  - Are they near or far away?
  - Are they supporting you from below like foundations, or are they balloons that lift you up?
  - What do you offer one another? What's the exchange?
  - Find your own way to map these spatially.

(This activity is adapted from Hawkins & Shohet (2007) *Getting the support and Supervision you need in Supervision in the Helping Professions.* Maidenhead: OUP)

Part Two

Projects for Groups & Creative Collaborations

Casey Bailey

Let Me Burn Your Page
and Show You the Ash

Collaboration can be a place for an artist to hide, or a place for an artist to be found. Within the walls of a collaborative piece work a poet can find a shelter that doesn't exist when working individually, but can also feel more exposed than ever. As a writer, I have become a serial collaborator, always treading a fine line between being terrified and enraptured by processes and outcomes that simply do not exist in creative isolation. The thing that has allowed me to embrace and enjoy a collaborative approach to creation is understanding why it is important to my practice and knowing how to get the most out of the partnership and how to give as much of myself to it as possible.

In his book *Collaboration in Art: from Conceptualism to Post Modernism*, Charles Green speaks on the way in which collaboration allows artists to separate themselves from the commonly held cliché of the artist as a lonely figure who awaits the arrival of inspiration. Green is referring specifically to the existence of the visual artist, but in many ways captures the perception of the poet, and the way in which collaboration can shatter this.

> Artistic collaboration is a special and obvious case of the manipulation of the figure of the artist, for at the very least collaboration involves a deliberately chosen alteration of artistic identity from individual to composite subjectivity. One expects new understandings of artistic authorship to appear in artistic collaborations, understandings that may or may not be consistent with the artists' solo productions before they take up collaborative projects.

An iamb of poets

A question that I often hear is what is the collective noun for poets? If you put yourself around poets enough, you are sure to hear some hilarious answers to this question. Perhaps my favourite answer to this question, though, is 'an iamb'. Having said this, I am sceptical as to whether you can find a group of poets where one in every two could be described as unstressed. Often in collaboration we really see this balance of stressed and unstressed (of course in a totally different context than the definition of iamb) within poets in a way that we rarely see in individuals. It is so common that poets experience, and even present, a sense of self doubt that we almost expect it of all who dance with the form. I can vividly remember hosting Terrence Hayes in Birmingham and listening to him open his reading by sharing that he hadn't memorised his poems as he hadn't written anything worthy of memorising yet. He was reading from the National Book Award-winning *American Sonnets for My Past and Future Assassin.* In his first poem, he referenced Sylvia Plath's self-doubt, questioning – *what do you call a visionary who does not recognise her vision?* And isn't this how it always goes: poets so skilled in the art of finding the fizz in the lemonade of each other's work, but seeing their own as flat and stale with those same eyes.

So what does this mean for collaboration? It means that the eyes on your work are not only doubled (or multiplied by whatever number exists within your collaboration), they are different. The first time I wrote collaboratively with a poet, with any real intent of creating something of merit, was in partnership with my very good friend Hannah Swingler. Hannah and I had taken on the task of performing a joint set of poetry at a poetry night, and were determined that some of the pieces would be a collaboration. I would argue that we entered that piece of work with more confidence than we had ever entered a piece or a project before. I had absolute confidence and Hannah had absolute confidence – in each other. Confidence in 50% of the writing is a much better situation than the confidence in 10% of the writing that I normally find myself in. Every time I shared something with Hannah I prefaced it with a comment about how poor it was, and was almost always greeted with praise beyond my expectations. On the flipside, Hannah kept sending me great poetry that was apparently 'unfinished' or 'not ready'. Leaning into each other in this way, and having faith in the opinion of a writer who I knew was at the peak of her powers, made it possible to free myself to just enjoy the process.

When Charley Barnes and Claire Walker collaborated to write *Hierarchy of Needs (A Retelling)*, the pamphlet, published by V. Press, existed in a different space to the collaborative performance that I had shared with Hannah, but the reciprocity and comradery are a definite parallel between the two. In a blog on collaboration, co-authored by Barnes and Walker, Barnes references the way that the pair supported each other through the process:

> Of course, with every writing project there are lows. There are the moments of, 'I just don't know that this is any good.' Collaborating has meant that these, too, have been shared though. When one has doubts, the other becomes the voice of reason. Fortunately, Claire and I have even managed to tag team this part of writing; when one begins to sink, the other becomes an airbelt.

In the resulting writing, we can see how poetry has become a three-way conversation, between poet, poet and reader. In the opening and closing poems of the pamphlet *Hierarchy of Needs (1)* and *Hierarchy of Needs (2)*, there are two rewritings of Maslow's Hierarchy of Needs that approach the same subject with a similar structure, but one driven very strongly by an extended botanical metaphor and one which feels like a much more direct address on the human condition. What I find fascinating about the pair is that the exact same line of poetry can exist in both and not only hold the poem together but also tie the two poems together.

Hierarchy of Needs (1)
(Extract)

Sunflowers will race; carnations will long to be
as beautiful; someone
is always choosing between
the prettiest

Hierarchy of Needs (2)
(Extract)

Competing against ourselves/everyone; like, follow;
share someone is
always choosing between the prettiest

As a reader, I'm not just arrested by the beauty of the writing and the reality of human nature that it captures, I'm intrigued by the process that allowed this pair of poems to come into existence. How does the same line sit so perfectly in two different poems? What does it do for each individual poem and what does it do for the pair? How did they land on it? I don't know that the answers to these questions necessarily matter but I know that they are part of the reason that I read both of these poems so many times and enjoyed them every time.

Images vs imagery

Images are the heart of poetry. You're not a poet without imagery.
(Anne Sexton)

A picture is a poem without words.
(Horace)

These quotes, often linked to Anne Sexton and Horace, provide us with a concise glimpse into the mutual bond between poetry and images, highlighting the interconnectedness between the two. But what happens when poems and images sit side by side? If a picture really says a thousand words, and our ability to write poetry is predicated by how well we conjure an image in someone's mind, can the combination of the two serve either?

The answer to this question surely lies in the work created and there are some truly stunning examples of collaboration featuring poetry and images to reference. Much like poetry and photography as stand alone art forms, there is no 'correct way' to bring images and poetry together. In Roger Robinson's stunning collaboration with Johny Pitts, *Home is Not a Place,* it feels like the photography and the words are together, unpicking and commenting on the same condition, although very often they are not in direct conversation with each other. There are also, however, many moments in the book where the photography and poetry feel more directly related. The poem 'Guy Fawkes Night' explores the role of a father in guiding his frightened son to a fireworks display and sits opposite a wonderful image of a firework exploding in the sky.

The approach taken by Liz Berry and Tom Hicks in their book *The Dereliction* feels slightly different. The poems and photographs fall into a very direct conversation with each other, with the inspiration for most of the poems immediately visible in the photograph it sits alongside. The poems do not describe the pictures to us, though, they somehow manage to expand them providing timelines, hidden scenes and personal stories. The photographs serve as beautiful anchors to the poems and portals from the poem back to the reality that it grew from.

Two books that take a different approach to collaboration, but find an excellent end product. There are many ways to do this well. But in the collaboration between image and imagery the role of the poem can never be to just describe the image. In Robinson's 'Guy Fawkes Night', he is not describing the fireworks that Pitts has captured in his photograph, but both the image and the words provide an additional insight into each other. In Berry's 'Secret Garden', she references drinking White Lightning, and, whilst there is no cheap cider present in the image, we can certainly see what David Attenborough would describe as its natural habitat. High equality mixed-media collaboration does not exist for one form to explain the other, but for them to meet somewhere new through play and exploration.

I'll bring the words

To collaborate with people who sit outside of the world of poetry is something that always inspires me to write in a different way and from a different place. This started for me when I was part of a program that paired artists from different disciplines and given one hour to create a piece. I was paired with a talented cellist – Megan Kirwin – and after a brief discussion I spent 40 minutes watching her play her cello, Arty, while I wrote a poem about him. Every now and then, I would share some of it with her and she would change how she was playing, sparking a whole new line of thought. This is still one of the most organic pieces of collaborative work that I have ever created, neither of us trying to steer the other, but still doing so merely by creating what we felt the work needed. It was many years later that I had one of those surreal experiences where you read something and know it to be true from an experience that you have already had. Writing on collaboration in his book *FreePlay: Improvisation in Life and Art*, Stephen Nachmanovich delineated how this type of collaboration works:

> The work comes from neither one artist nor the other, even though our own idiosyncrasies and styles, the symptoms of our original natures, still exert their natural pull. Nor does the work come from a compromise or halfway point (averages are always boring!), but from a third place that isn't necessarily like what either one of us would do individually. What comes is a revelation to both of us. There is a third, totally new style that pulls on us.

For me, this experience of collaboration set me on a journey of seeking out opportunities to work with others. This has led me to collaborate as a writer with other writers, to write the poetry for a ballet produced with the Birmingham Royal Ballet, to curate and write for a show with the BBC Symphony Orchestra and to continue to seek collaboration wherever I may find it. Throughout these experiences I have learnt to hold onto ideas that appear to sit in opposition with each other, but that always guide my approach to collaboration.

Be vulnerable

To achieve new heights and enter new spaces with your poetry, you have to be vulnerable, you have to embrace the potential for things to be difficult and for you to create something that isn't perfect. Allow yourself to be open to other people's eyes on your work during this process, embrace the fear that they are going to see it before you are ready but that is only going to help in getting it ready. Be excited about the potential criticism, remember that you are working together, so the person feeding back to you is as invested in making great work as you are. This doesn't mean that they are always right, but you can trust in their intentions, they are working with you to create, not against you.

Be secure

There are two very simple facts for you to know when you are collaborating. The first is that you are there because you bring something, it will be different to other people but it is important and will play an essential role in shaping the final work. The second is that you do not bring everything, so when there is a lull or a break in inspiration, you can lean on the people you are working with to provide that burst of energy.

I always try to carry the idea that I have to be both vulnerable and secure into any collaborative exercise that I do, and I would strongly suggest that you take that same attitude into your collaborations.

ACTIVITY: Out of frame – an exercise in inspiration and collaboration

The first part of this activity is a simple one that many writers will have completed before and can be completed in isolation:

Step 1: Out of frame
- Use any image of your choosing and write a description of everything that you think is happening out of frame; this could focus on one side of the image, what's happening behind a door or even what is happening with the photographer/artist.
- Using imagery captured from within the image, write a poem focused specifically on what is happening out of frame, without directly explaining what you can see.

Step 2: In the frame
- Complete step one at the same time as a fellow poet. When you have completed your poems, exchange them.
- Your new role is to write a poem about what exists inside the frame. What is happening in the image that you cannot see, based on the out of frame poem from your partner? The ideal outcome is not to be correct, it is to be inspired.

Works Cited:

Stephen Nachmanovich (1990) *FreePlay: Improvisation in Life and Art,* Jeremy P Tarcher.

Charles Green (2000) *Collaboration in Art from Conceptualism to Post Modernism,* University of New South Wales Press.

Charley Barnes and Claire Walker (2021) *In Praise of Collaboration* http://www.charleybarneswriter.com/blog/in-praise-of-collaboration-by-charley-barnes-and-claire-walker

Roger Robinson, Johny Pitts (2022) *Home is Not a Place,* Harper Collins.

Liz Berry and Tom Hicks (2021) The Dereliction, Hercules Editions.

Charley Barnes and Claire Walker (2021) *Hierarchy of Needs: A Retelling.* V Press.

Jasmine Gardosi

Working with Music:
Ten Things I've Learnt

Let's start off with a secret. I HATED collaborating. Just couldn't do it. I'd tried. I'd already taken part in projects that required working with other artists – most notably, one where I was asked to come up with "the best poem I've ever written" within a week, in the corner of a dance studio. Some people thrive in those conditions. I don't. When I'm on the spot, the stuff I make sucks. I hate what I write in workshops. I find freestyling hard. I can't jam. In ways, I'm too precious and too much of a control freak to work with other people – an introverted ball of perfectionism whose best work is premeditated. I felt consigned to work alone forever.

Then I encountered music. I was asked by Jack Crowe to feature at his new jazz/poetry crossover night based in Digbeth, Birmingham, called Funkenteleky. Here, poets were prompted to perform with the backing of the Ben Lee quintet. In the past, I'd been awed by Tongue Fu, a genre-leading show headed by Chris Redmond, which combines poetry and music in a similar way – but I'd never *done* anything like that. As a chronic non-collaborator, I was apprehensive.

As a feature poet for Funkenteleky, I was asked to write a 'poetry map' – which involved taking a printed poem, and scribbling all over it in coloured felt tip to illustrate what I wanted the music to do. The idea was that the musicians would figure it out from there. I was nervous, I was uncertain, but I preferred this to being asked to create a poem on the spot. I could at least plan some elements. What I didn't plan for was stepping on stage and being rudely awoken – in the best possible way – by the brass section when it kicked in during my poem. It brought me alive. Music became a possibility – an infinite, colourful tool with which to experiment and aid performance. For the first time, collaboration came easy for me. It made sense.

I'd like to share ten lessons I learnt since this moment, and take you through my journey from chronic non-collaborator stifled by perfectionism to the leader of a six-piece Celtic Dubstep band that tours nationally. Whatever your creative hopes and dreams, I hope you can take some inspiration from them.

1. Yes, the musicians *do* want to work with you

It's easy for us as poets to feel insecure about our abilities as artists. What do we offer, *really*, other than some self-indulgent words? Anyone can do that. Whereas musicians? They're magicians conjuring sound colour out of instruments, using *their* skills to lift *us* up. If you've wanted to work with musicians but have felt shy because of this – I get it.

Gratitude is always helpful but imposter syndrome less so. It took me a while to consider that there is actually mutual admiration – that the musicians appreciate what we as poets do. If you're feeling insecure about working with musicians or practitioners of any other art form, I invite you to consider that maybe, like spiders, they might be even more scared of your skill with words than you are of their musical abilities. The Funkenteleky musicians made it clear the respect was mutual, despite them being so generous with their talents. It felt the same with the musicians involved in Musical Mouthpieces, another poetry/music crossover event run by Joe Cook at which I was also invited to perform. These were generous people who don't just serve the poet, but the common cause of music. For some, combining poetry and music is an exciting and refreshing prospect. You're not boring them and you're not wasting their time.

There are lots of beautiful musicians out there. Not everyone you meet will be keen, but put yourself in the way of more and more musicians and eventually you will cross paths with people who align with your vision and will want to spend more time working with you. They might even recommend other collaborators from the music communities they themselves are plugged into, who they sense will fit your vibe.

2. No, you don't have to rap

Rhythmic poetry is great. I dig it. I write and perform a lot of it. But if you're working with music, you don't *need* this. Personally, poetry that addresses an audience outside of the rhythm, that doesn't fall regularly on the beat, actually arrests my attention more. Take Baz Luhrman's 'The Sunscreen Song' or even 'The revolution will not be televised' by Gill Scott Heron. Like me, you might find that polysyllabic rhyming doesn't come naturally to you. You don't need it to. In fact, your words may stand out more without a strict rhythm, or rhyming. My poetry/music pieces are a mixture of strictly rhythmic pieces, arhythmic pieces, conversational pieces following natural dialogue/speech, and even pieces where my speech *fights* against the rhythm of the instruments. So I offer you to give yourself permission to play with different rhythms and see what comes out, much in the same way we can use form to push ourselves into new creative zones. Conversational rhythm? Soundscape with no beat? Tight, regular bars? It's up to you.

3. Silence is a power

You're got music, and you're not afraid you use it. Great. But in the same way the most important line of your poem is sometimes better delivered as a whisper rather than a shout, when working with music, you don't need the intensity of sound to lift that same line. And on a wholly practical level, the louder the volume, the greater the risk that this same momentous line of poetry gets drowned out.

When performing my own poems with music, I often ask the musicians to pause whatever they're playing just before the most important line, so that I can deliver it in silence. The sharper the contrast, the more impactful. And you *do* have control over this element if you're working with musicians. Instrumentalists are brilliant listeners and watchers. If you gesture for them to stop, they will find the stop in the music. Similarly, if you gesture for them to lower their volume, or raise it, then they will. Play with the live dynamics. You are in control.

4. Give the music even more to do

After the high of performing at Funkenteleky and Musical Mouthpieces, I realised I wanted to explore the possibilities of music fully. I applied to and was successful in receiving a Developing Your Creative Practice Grant from Arts Council England, which funded me to combine music and poetry in more exploratory ways. I was less interested in directly laying music over poetry as a backing track or accompaniment, because I'd done it and seen it done lots of times and I wanted to try something different. I wanted to fuse the elements on a more fundamental level. How could I create pieces where the poetry *needed* the music for it to make sense? Where one couldn't exist without the other? Where the music is somehow part of the story of the poem? I wanted to directly interact with the instruments, not just let them be an accompaniment. I wanted to converse with the musicians, to argue, to interrupt, to be drowned out by them. The funding meant I could pay musicians to lock themselves in a rehearsal room with me and try *all* of this silly stuff out.

That's how poems like 'Your Silence Sounds Like' came about. It's a piece about receiving the silent treatment, and I use the band as a ticking bomb that explodes into a dubstep drop. Here's how the poem's pivotal moment looks on the page:

And then your silence. Your silence sounds like…

[the music drops]

That's it. I don't complete that simile – at least, not with words. The bass line does that for the audience, as it hits their guts. Working with music allowed me to practise the age-old 'show don't tell', but showing it with *music* instead.

I like this poem because I literally cannot perform it without music. For me, that's the ultimate method of combining content with form. You don't *have* to, but I find it a fun prompt to ask the question: "If I can perform this poem without music, are you *really* making the most use of it?"

Another example of entwining the roles of music and words tightly in a piece is a poem titled 'B or G'. I use the endless, infinite scale of musical notes as an extended metaphor to demonstrate my own interpretation of gender. The set-up is an argument between me and a pianist. Assuming an imposing, transphobic character, I respond with frustration to the pianist who toggles between playing two notes: 'B' or 'G':

[pianist plays a B]

That's a B... You're a... B. Yah?

[pianist plays a G]

Oh – are you a G?

[pianist plays a B]

B

[pianist plays a G]

or a G

Which one are you?

[pianist plays a B]

Okay. You're a B.

[*pianist plays a G*]

No, you're a G.

At this point, the pianist starts to introduce other notes into the song, aside from 'B' and 'G'. An 'A' for example.

"It's one or the other." I respond

The pianist then plays 'G', 'A', then 'B'.

"There's no in between", I protest.

The pianist then plays a scale including a host of other notes.

"No no, there is no spectrum. There is no scale." I hit back.

The pianist breaks out into further notes, building a beautifully expressive song – until I shoot it down in response:

All other notes disgust me.
It's simple science
The world is made up of B or G.
All we have is B or G
And a B is a B
And a G is a G

You can see I've used the extended metaphor of notes on a scale to demonstrate that much like music, nothing in life, let alone gender, exists in a binary.

The musical scale as an analogy for the infinite spectrum of gender expression is just one parallel you can draw between music and a subject you feel deeply about. The way your stomach drops when a heavy bass line hits (like in 'Your Silence Sounds Like' is another.) There are limitless comparisons that can be drawn between the multi-faceted elements of music and your own subjects that you want to explore. I invite you to have fun with them.

5. It's okay not to have the words...

... because you can use the music, instead. It might be there's a sentiment, a problem or the faintest of ideas kicking about in the bottom of your mind, that hasn't even made it to draft stage because you don't know how to articulate the thought – or because you don't know the answers to it yet. I'd like to talk about how I used music to push through this rut with one of my own pieces.

'Jas + Sax' is a conversation between me and a saxophonist. The script starts off like this – my words are on the left-hand side, the saxophonist's response is on the right:

Hey. Can I ask you something?

brass

should I tell my students I'm gay?

brass

okay yeah but
 it's not as simple as that

brass?

I don't really know the exact words that the saxophone is 'saying' in response to my questions – but I don't need to. The audience gets the gist.

It reminds me of a virtual UniSlam seminar during lockdown, where Paul Tran invited us, the participants, to begin writing a new poem with the thought: *suppose I was wrong?* I needed this permission to not have to know everything when writing a piece. I have a bad habit of end-gaming in my poems, where I need to know the answer clearly before I commit effort to it. But when the saxophone is the one with the answer, you don't need the words. The poem ends like this:

what if they lose trust in me?

what if they don't want to come to the poetry club anymore,

because I'm an icky gay?

brass

yeah, but –

brass

… no, you don't understand…

* brass!

brass!

brass!*

…. I see your point.

I didn't need to verbally articulate the 'moral' or the 'wisdom' of the piece – I handed it over to the musician. It was a relief. The *saxophone* held the answers, which didn't have to exist in the English language. I'd call a poem written in this style a kind of vignette. There is relatively little of the whole conversation shown, but you, the audience, fill in the gaps with your own imagination.

Leaving the poem 'unfinished' in this way was freeing. Gone was the perfectionist impulse. I *couldn't* bring a perfect/flawless poem with all its bells and whistles to the rehearsal room, because the saxophone *had* to complete it.

Isn't that incredible? That as a poet, you can quite deliberately aim for 'unfinished' when you're collaborating. The gaps *are* the strength so give your collaborators – whether they are musicians, dancers, singers, or another poet – a chance to do their thing in those gaps. The answers might present themselves without you realising.

6. Let go of cleverness, find authenticity

This freedom from perfectionism took me out of 'must write a perfect poem' and into 'let's play!' Just as importantly, it also allowed a space for vulnerability. It wasn't about 'writing a poem'. There is so little conventional 'poetic technique' in 'Jas + Sax' because I trust the conceit – the fact I'm talking metaphorically to a saxophone – to be the 'poetry' of the piece. I focused less on being clever, and more about telling a truth.

That's why the following lines were able to come out in 'Jas + Sax Part II' which follows a similar format. In this piece, I ask the saxophone whether I should tell my parents about my gender identity:

> I would rather wait for my whole family to die
> before I explore being trans.
>
> **brass**
>
> That's how I've envisioned myself
> the most free from shame.
>
> **brass**
>
> Thanks.

I wasn't trying to write a poem, or keep to a metre, or honour a metaphor, or rhyme. It's pure unfiltered speech, straight from the source. Trusting that the music will be the art of the piece allowed me to be raw with my words, and gave me the courage to lean into this subject matter.

I provide this example to invite you to use music to take you out of a place of 'be clever' and into a place of 'be authentic'. Another prompt: take your frankest poem, or a truth of yours that is *so* stripped back and simple, you don't even see it as a poem – and see what happens when you add music to it. Music can become a safeguard for vulnerability, an aid, a tool. Don't worry about entertaining your audience, or being clever, or poetic. They are engaged. You are safe. Tell your truth.

7. Be a beginner

And about vulnerability – it's okay to suck at something. And suck I did. At the same time as slowly discovering the possibilities of music, I was becoming obsessed with the art form of beatboxing from watching it on YouTube, and I wanted to learn how to do it. I'd heard pioneering beatboxers like Rahzel singing lyrics at the same time as beatboxing:

b If your *pff*mother *bb* on-*b**pff*-ly knew

This dude was singing the lyrics "If your mother only knew" whilst honouring his beat of "b *pff* b b b pft". I was impressed. It sounded impossible. And I'd wondered – what would happen if I, a poet, tried the same thing, but made it easier for myself by using my strength with words to write the beat *into* the letters of the lyrics, using words that contained the plosive letters 'b' and 'p'?

I had *one* poem idea in mind, and that drove me to apply for a Jerwood Arts Bursary that would fund me to get coaching from a beatboxer. I was accepted, and just like that, Jerwood changed my career. It took a long time, though. A coach meant my technique was kept on track, but gosh, I sucked. It's uncomfortable being a beginner. As artists, we spend a lot of time wanting to exit the vulnerable space of being a beginner – being 'not that good' at something. Could I dare be rubbish at something? In ways, I felt fortunate – I started my beatbox coaching in lockdown so was relatively tucked away. I could practice in private because that's the only place I existed.

After nine months of trial and error, 'Be Poet' came out. It used my strengths as a wordsmith to weave the beat into the words so that I could beatbox and speak at the same time. I used 'b' and 'p' words alliteratively to imitate a heartbeat, delivering each one with the strong punch of a kickdrum I'd learnt through beatbox coaching:

We people
we problems
we babble
like babies
til purple
then playback
the blabber
then blubber
at bumbles
we perspire
then bubble
then pulp up
like paper
we're paupers
of blood pressure

I'm still learning to be better at beatboxing. I will never be like the absolute heroes you can find on YouTube and Grand Beatbox Battle. My saving grace is that I can weave it with poetry in a new way. So, like with any new skill (or musical accompaniment) you want to add to your arsenal, remember you don't have to be the best at it – your USP is that you're combining it with poetry.

8. You don't need a full band. Just one musician is enough
I'm fortunate that I had the means to work with full bands. That is down to visionary hosts and organisers like Jack Crowe and Joe Cook who facilitated musicians for their poetry events, and also down to Arts Council England who gave me funds to get

world-class musicians in one room at the same time. But there are other ways of doing this. Working with one musician (hell, even a friend who plays an instrument, they don't have to be 'professional') is a great way to go, as long as there is trust and enthusiasm and space for you both to flourish. I've seen this work beautifully. There is a specialness in duets like these. Kamil Mahmood and Aayushi is one example of two artists with a common cause who write songs/poems together. The power is in the intimacy of the performance.

9. You don't need to have a band at all.
Just you, the poet, is enough – even if you're not a John Hegley with his ukulele, or Hannah Silva with her loop pedal. We can use the tools we have at our disposal for delivery, e.g. volume, speed, pacing – these are our instruments. Use a beat on your chest, click, use the *audience* as your band by directing them to keep the rhythm, or sing. You can even use beatboxing. There is music available to you, even if other people – and their instruments – aren't.

10. Trust
The result of this all exploration was 'Dancing To Music You Hate', a poetry, beatbox and Celtic Dubstep show about gender identity. It was a compilation of all of these experiments, which naturally followed a thread that explored gender identity because that was what I was principally writing about at the time. It's also the most authentic piece of work I've ever created. In another of my poems, 'Jas vs. Ad Space', I confess how, during the isolation of lockdown,

> My gender identity was around *every* corner of the house.
> I cried for hours over Trans TikTok compilations.
> I saw myself in my own thoughts, for once.

The first time I uttered words like these was to my bandmates in the rehearsal room. They might not have made it out further had my bandmates not heard, validated and supported them.

The musicians weren't just accompaniments on-stage – on a more fundamental level, they helped articulate my story by hearing and supporting it first. I'm not sure what would have happened to 'B or G' if my pianist Jobe Sullivan hadn't turned around to me and said "That's my favourite poem of yours" after he'd first heard it.

Both musically and thematically, the show was a product of trust – the musicians trusting that I was onto something, and helping support that. It was also a product of the trust of Andrew Fletcher who commissioned me to make the show when he worked for Warwick Arts Centre. Trust is the greatest creative lubricant. The poetry I make when I feel believed in is my best stuff. I imagine it's the same for you.

Working with musicians has taught me a few things – but, above all, I've learnt that if you're surrounding yourself with collaborators, try to make sure you can see mutual trust being built. Creating such an environment doesn't manage to happen all the time, so don't blame yourself if the creativity is a little different when the trust isn't quite there. But when it is, you're flying.

Damn. Maybe collaborating isn't so bad after all.

ACTIVITY

Using the extracts of 'Jas + Sax' as an example, write a dialogue between you and an instrument – your words on the left hand of the page, the instrument on the right.

Steps:

1. Think of a conversation you'd like to have in which you are telling a truth, e.g. asking for advice on a difficult subject (coming out to your students, say), or expressing something difficult for the first time, or asking an impossible favour. Maybe it's giving someone a piece of your mind (something that you've always wanted to get off your chest) or having an argument with someone.

2. For further inspiration, think of who the instrument represents – who you're having a conversation with. This can be with someone in particular in mind – a friend you talk to all the time, or someone you can *never* talk to – a well-known figure (Donald Trump, maybe?), or someone no longer in your life. It also doesn't have to be anyone in particular – just some abstract 'friend' who somehow has all the answers.

3. Write *your* side of the dialogue on the left-hand side of the page. On the right, write 'brass' or 'strings' or 'music' – no words. You can add inflections or punctuation to determine the tone or insinuate the gist of what the instrument is saying, but no words, e.g. "Brass?" "Brass!"

4. Enjoy the freedom this offers. Allow yourself to focus on the truth that *you* say in your dialogue. Don't worry about being 'poetic' – the poetry is already there in the conceit.

Gregory Leadbetter

Poetry, Photography, and the Making of *Balanuve*

Poetry is often regarded as a solitary art, but however solitary the experience of composition and reading might be – and neither necessarily are – poetry, like all the arts, participates actively in the world that it feeds and is fed by. As language, its essence is communicative, not sequestered: poetry seeks to connect, to take up and transform, to utter and be uttered, to affect and be affected. It is an omnivorous, multivalent, promiscuous art. As such, its collaborations – broadly conceived – can be so implicit and naturalised to the medium as to go all but unnoticed, or pass as allusion or other kinds of intertextuality. At times, however, its relationship to other art forms is foregrounded as central to the character of the work that emerges, as in the book of poems and photographs published as *Balanuve* by Broken Sleep Books in 2021. I wrote the poems in 2015; the photographs had been taken by Phil Thomson in Dundee over the course of one month in 1968. How then did this project – and its eventual realisation not only as a book, but as a work of audio-visual poetry theatre, with a soundtrack by Tom Tebby – come about, and what exactly is it?

Balanuve has its origins in a conversation about poetry and photography. In 2015, Thomson held an exhibition called *mono 68*, featuring the striking black and white monochrome photographs from which I would eventually choose the twenty-four images included and arranged, each accompanied by a poem, in *Balanuve*. (You can see the first poem and photograph in the sequence at the end of this essay.) Thomson and I were colleagues at Birmingham City University at the time, and I was lucky enough to attend the private view of his exhibition when it was hosted there. It made a strong impression on me, and together – quite casually – we floated the idea that I might write a series of poems that responded in some way to some of the photographs. Thomson himself is a poet, lyricist, and graphic artist, as well as photographer, so he is no stranger to the curious relays that run between differing art forms. Neither of us had any idea what, if anything, would develop as a result, but we were both intrigued by the possibilities. Thomson handed me around ninety prints to take away.

For some weeks I spent time, when I could, simply contemplating the photographs. This was in effect my own, truly private view of the images that Thomson had captured as a student at Duncan of Jordanstone College of Art nearly fifty years before. I didn't know Dundee, nor have any personal connection to the city. As a British child of the mid-seventies, many scenes were not so very alien to me, but a spatio-temporal divide was nonetheless palpable: they felt like photographs of a vanished world – a world that my parents and grandparents might have known, but I did not.

I found that spatio-temporal rift – the relation between the there/then of the photographs and the here/now of my mediatory imagination and historical perspective – creatively fertile. I started to envision the photographs as images not of the actual world we inhabit, but of another world – one very like, but also radically different to my own: a weird double of Britain, with a counterfactual history. Once I started to see that world, that country and its whole society clearly, certain images became particularly salient – and imaginatively radiant – as revelatory expressions of that history. The imaginary city of Balanuve (I'll come back to its name) emerged complete from my contemplation of those images. It had developed like a photograph in the darkroom of my imagination, and emotionally engrossed me. I recognised, by the vividness of this experience, that something within me was trying to get written. It was, evidently, ready to manifest, and in this process had found its form and its moment.

In the tale of this imaginary city, I saw that, however obliquely, the poems and their story-world addressed not just a British context, but issues of urgent global concern, that filled – and continue to fill – the news (and often preoccupied me): urban desolation, environmental damage, displacement and migration, nationalism, conflict and its victims, state authority and the abuse of state power – and the quirks, unevenness, and unexpectedness of social, spatial and cultural renewal, in relation to its intentions. From these emerged further themes fundamental to the work: the relationship between history and cultural amnesia, society and education, science and wisdom, art and action, ruin and myth.

As I composed *Balanuve*, I found my imagination taking up all kinds of material from the lumber room of my knowledge and experience and incorporating them, quite organically, into the fabric of its making: historical legislation like the Act of Indemnity and Oblivion, the Wars of the Three Kingdoms, medieval Arthurian romance, Heraclitean philosophy, Chaucer's *Canterbury Tales*, consumer brands, war slogans, modern political soundbites, Hitchcock films, art history, the Bible, etymology, and repurposed acronyms, to name some – anything somehow spontaneously useful in conjuring this weird counterfactual double of Britain into being. I conceived each poem and its accompanying photograph as a chapter in the story of Balanuve. The synthesis of familiarity and unfamiliarity – ostensibly recognisable scenes infused with a different narrative – combined with the peculiar matrix of its materials, both visual and poematic, produced a work of the urban uncanny, at once a 'history' and a mystery. I called my imaginary city Balanuve – pronounced 'ba-la-noov', with the emphasis on the long final syllable: an anglicisation of *baile naomh*, Scots Gaelic for 'holy city' – in honour of the real city and people of Dundee imaged so evocatively in Thomson's photographs. I wrote a simple prologue to the book, to prime the reader for the sequence that followed:

> These poems and photographs tell the story of a city: Balanuve.
> This city is in Britain, but it might be anywhere.
> The story begins with the mysterious death of Balanuve.
> It is devastated and abandoned.
> In time, people return. A new society takes shape and
>   begins to thrive.
> The city is rebuilt, but things go wrong. New threats emerge.
> Balanuve must again renew itself, if it is to survive.

Balanuve, then, is a different kind of creature to other books of poetry and photography such as *Positives* by Thom Gunn and his brother Ander (1966), *Remains of Elmet* by Ted Hughes and Fay Godwin (1979), and *The Dereliction* by Liz Berry and Tom Hicks, which was published the same year as *Balanuve* (2021). It is not strictly 'ekphrastic' poetry, in its modern sense, either, as it does not seek to describe a work of visual art external to the poem. (Incidentally, there is something in Don Paterson's remark that today – divorced as it is from its origins in Classical rhetoric – "ekphrastic poetry" is "almost as arbitrary a genre as 'poetry about animals'".) While each photograph is presented in concert with its accompanying poem, the relationship between the two is oblique rather than descriptive. The poem does not attempt to represent the photograph, but to set it in a fresh imaginative context.

There is a very long debate in aesthetics and poetics – not least in response to Horace's analogy, *ut pictura poesis* ("as painting is, so is poetry") – that considers the relation between verbal and visual art. Gotthold Lessing argued in the eighteenth century that this analogy does not hold, given the formal differences between the arts, and that as such, strictly speaking, ekphrasis is both unachievable and undesirable: form *is* content, and the verbal and the visual arts, while kindred and complimentary, tangle with our psychophysiology in differing ways. In so doing, he highlighted characteristics of poetry that Philip Sidney and Ben Jonson had also emphasised in this debate: while the poem is "a representing, counterfeiting, or figuring forth," as Sidney puts it, a poem is not *just* a picture, but – as a form of words – also addresses what Jonson calls the 'understanding', i.e. concept, logic, grammar. By using and addressing the organ of language itself, poetry involves effects not limited to the visual.

I did not seek to 'paint pictures', then, in the poems of *Balanuve*, nor to compete with the unique virtues of the picture – in this case, the photograph – as an art form. The principle involved is closer to that of *enargeia*, to use another term from the aesthetic debate (discussed by Aristotle, Dionysius of Halicarnassus, Quintilian, Longinus, and other ancient thinkers): a sensuous evocation in language that, in its effects, makes the reader a kind of emotionally engaged eyewitness to the imaginary. While presented alongside the photographs with which they were paired – the double-action that distinguishes the form of the book – the poems had also to stand alone, and persuade on their own terms. Moreover, it is upon the poems that the "willing suspension of disbelief" (in Coleridge's phrase) necessary for the reader to access Balanuve depends: the photographs *alone* do not (and could not) create Balanuve. The poems are the reader's psychagogues for the imaginary city, and the creative agents of its reality-effect. As Longinus says, "the object of poetry is to enthral" – and the poems at once constitute the vision and act as its spectral guide.

The poems therefore *activate* the photographs with which they are presented in particular ways – just as my contemplation of the photographs activated my imagination in ways that responded to the evocative power of the images themselves, and that "illogical conjunction" of "spatial immediacy and temporal

127

anteriority" that Roland Barthes identifies as characteristic of photography. Poem and image exist in mutually inductive relationship, both creatively, for the poet, and experientially, for the reader. The distinctive kinds of interiority that each art form offers – the image-transcending, ordering, animating power of language, and the cognitive immediacy of the image – interact in the composition of the work as a whole.

A photograph is a kind of fragment – a pattern of light and shade imprinted from a transitory reality – and I was conscious of composing the story of Balanuve in and by fragments. This fragmentary quality in turn corresponded to the nature of a ruin, which felt appropriate to the nature of Balanuve as a ruined city. A fragment is always suggestive, and just as a photograph embodies a synecdochic relation – in which we see a world through a part, and a part through a world, in one and the same moment – so I conceived Balanuve as a work of archaeological, reconstructive imagination. Certain characters in the story also encounter the city and what they find there in a similar way – though the reader, granted a privileged ironic perspective, can see that those characters do not always come to the 'right' conclusions in the face of the evidence (while nevertheless finding something affectively and cognitively *real* in the very act of inquiry and speculation). Balanuve and its story (and stories within that story) emerges from the gaps in knowledge – the productive *un*knowing – that fragmentariness and its epistemological reflex involves. As a narrative, I came to think of *Balanuve* as an experiment in elliptical epic – a vast story, played out over an unspecified span of time – seen by glimpses, in and through the poems and photographs.

Both the demotic and often quite eerie qualities captured in Thomson's photographs also suggested, to me, the kind of 'voice' that I wanted the poems to assume: a voice at once somewhat vatic and close to the vernacular, both intimate and distant, knowing and unknowing – observational, anecdotal, contingent, and proceeding by visionary instantiation, rather than comfortably omniscient. Again, the verbal character of the poems speaks from and to the gaps and uncertainties fundamental the narrative. I also drew on the resources of conversational English partly to accentuate a sense of double exposure to both the familiar and the unfamiliar. Double exposures of various kinds run through the sequence, in fact: absence and presence, dystopia and utopia, seriousness and humour, scepticism and hope – each acting as the organ of the other. The monochrome form of the photographs also prompted me to invest in the poems that quality of elusive temporality – and uncanny simultaneity – which again became a function of poetic voice. I used allusion and the possibilities of anachronistic collocation as a way of wiring the circuit of the story up to actual historical or imaginative narratives, both to connect Balanuve to our world and to distance it from it – the better to see both that world and this.

That focus on scene, not self – a poetic impersonality – became analogous to the impersonality of the camera, for me: the eye not the I, in which the maker is implicit, at once hidden and active, in the picture or the fiction they create. I wanted *Balanuve* to enact a seeing of seeing – a watching of world-making – and in this, the interactive syntax of word and image, which draws heightened attention to that act, was fundamental. This kind of 'seeing' – in which both poet and photographer, naturally and unselfconsciously, are 'seers' – is essentially mythic in character, and exposes the foundational imaginative medium by which we apprehend, name, and constitute our reality. *Balanuve* is, amongst other things, a study in that process, and an assertion of its political and ethical significance for us all.

The Funeral

It begins with a funeral –
the dead city laid in its Sunday best
under bleached-white cloud.
Its people are shadows pinned to the road.
They have come out to see this last parade
of Andalusian black and wedding-day light.
The undertakers in top hats, tails and shades
carry the cardboard coffin and the weightless cargo
of the city's soul, shaking cans,
collecting for the ferryman
and the cold promise of escape.
Only one bearer is honestly sad, eyeing the children
who wait so well-behaved
for a float to bring music and sweets,
while the grown-ups, afraid, revert to blind reflex
and clump at a church. It is locked.
The dismantling of the high-rise
is half-way done, and the chimneys of last century
line up for absolution.
Those who oversee the end
are young: they have made
their final ritual
fun.

from *Balanuve* (Broken Sleep Books, 2021)

Photograph credit: Phil Thomson

ACTIVITY:

Find a group of photographs and write an asynchronous collaboration of your own.

Ideally, use photographs taken by someone else: I found the fact that I hadn't taken the pictures I used in *Balanuve* imaginatively liberating. That distance is enabling.

Invent a story-world that links the photographs, as a sequence. Imagine those photographs – whatever their actual provenance – are of that otherworld that you have invented.

Invest those photographs with an entirely new imaginary space-time, in and through your poems.

Look for details in the photographs that you can use in defamiliarising ways, in your poems – so that you create a correspondence between the detail of the poem and the detail of the image.

Attend closely to your own imaginative and emotional responses to the photographs – so that you try to become aware of qualities and particulars in the images that the eye might have noticed, but the conscious mind might have been slower to recognise. Use these insights, feelings and perceptions – however strange – in the making of your sequence of poems.

Works Cited:

Barthes, Roland, 'The Rhetoric of the Image', in *Image, Music, Text*, trs. Stephen Heath (Hill and Wang, 1977)

Berry, Liz and Tom Hicks, *The Dereliction* (Hercules Editions, 2021)

Coleridge, Samuel Taylor, *Biographia Literaria*, ed. James Engell and W. Jackson Bate, 2 vols (Princeton University Press, 1983)

Greene, Roland, S. Cushman *et al* (eds.), *The Princeton Encyclopedia of Poetry and Poetics*, 4th edn. (Princeton University Press, 2012)

Gunn, Thom and Ander Gunn, *Positives* (Faber & Faber, 1966)

Horace, *Ars Poetica* [https://www.poetryfoundation.org/articles/69381/ars-poetica]

Hughes, Ted and Fay Godwin, *Remains of Elmet* (Faber & Faber, 1979)

Jonson, Ben, *Discoveries made upon Men and Matter*, ed. Henry Morley (Cassell, 1892)

Leadbetter, Gregory and Phil Thomson, *Balanuve* (Broken Sleep Books, 2021)

Lessing, Gotthold Ephraim, *Laocoön: An Essay on the Limits of Painting and Poetry*, trs. Edward Allen McCormick (1766; Johns Hopkins University Press, 1984)

Longinus, *On the Sublime*, trs. James A. Arieti and John M. Crossett (Edwin Mellen Press, 1985)

Paterson, Don, *The Poem: Lyric, Sign, Metre* (Faber & Faber, 2018)

Sidney, Philip, *An Apology for Poetry*, ed. Geoffrey Shepherd (Manchester University Press, 1973)

Helen Ivory

The Poetry Feedback Group

Writing a poem goes through many stages. First, it's an unformed creature in your head. Then comes the summoning, when you sit down to write, and it is shaped by ink or pixels into words and tries to stand up on its own. But it's not ready yet, so you give it a heart and some breath for its lungs and hold it while it takes its first steps. You look at each other for a bit. You steady its gait and unfuzzy its edges. Is it able to stand on its own? How would you know? Perhaps you need more pairs of eyes.

As a writer of poems, I find it hard not to think of a poem as a living thing. A poem is part of me, it comes from me, but at the same time it is not me. To look objectively at a poem is the first step towards editing, and the next step along, I have found, is to seek the opinion of other people who write poems and know what you're up to. I am lucky enough to have always been part of a poetry feedback group. First when I was a student, then when my tutor George Szirtes started one up for us graduates. We have carried on these past fifteen years on our own, with some of the same core members plus a few newer people who have the same level of writing experience. We are each other's first audience and respect each other's practice.

The most important thing about a poetry feedback group is that you are all there for the sake of the poems. It is a community of poets who read, critique, and question each other's work. Writing poems can feel like a lonely experience when it is just you and your poem sitting in a room. Sitting in a circle of people who are also engaged in this process will reassure you that you are not alone in what sometimes can feel like a struggle. It can also make you feel what you're doing is valid, especially if you know no other writers apart from your group.

Time to get practical. What follows is a series of questions which I imagine you might have at this stage, if you are not already part of a poetry feedback group. I will then offer some answers and also a guideline on etiquette for such groups. I hope you find this useful.

How do I find a poetry feedback group?

Pre-internet, you needed to be in a physical space to meet other poets – now, there are also search engines and social media to make connections. If you live remotely, or if you have access issues, as long as you have reasonable broadband you should be able to find a poetry community. Since the pandemic, the world has opened up to live online events and people from all over the world can meet together to listen to and discuss poetry.

Many people who are currently part of feedback groups began by joining a Poetry Society 'Stanza' group. It's worth looking on the website to see what provision is in your area. If there is not a Stanza group in your area, you can start one and become a Stanza Rep, which will put you in contact with other poets in your area. Likewise, if the one in your area is oversubscribed already, you can create another. Another way of forming a feedback group is doing a course either online or in person and continuing to meet with other participants afterwards. Quite a few people who have done online courses with me over the years have formed small feedback groups. Another way is to just be in the 'zone'. Go to poetry events and get to know other poets and start something yourself. It helps to be proactive and to think of yourself as a writer; that this is part of your identity, and you are serious about what you do and what you want to do.

What are the practicalities of a poetry feedback group?

There are two types of groups – one led by a workshop leader, and one run by peers. We are going to focus here on the latter. The ideal number of people for such a group is four to eight people. This is working on the basis that a session lasts two to three hours, and you meet once a month. There needs to be sufficient time to spend on each of your poems. Some groups will take it in turns to bring poems to the sessions, in others everyone brings in a poem each time. Poems are sent out a few days in advance of the workshop, so everybody has a chance to read them before the session.

If this is an in-person group, you will need to either hire or borrow a space or run the sessions in one of the participant's houses. Some groups take turns to host. For online groups, Zoom or Skype seem to be the best platform for this type of activity. Some groups use email, and never actually meet in real time at all – there are many ways you can make this work.

What happens during a poetry feedback session?
This is both a social and focused occasion which can begin with tea, wine, or whatever makes people feel at home. With my own group, we usually chat about poetry/life related things around my kitchen table until everyone settles in. Because people rarely volunteer to go first, we do our version of 'spin the bottle' which decides the poem order. The poet will then read their poem, and everyone will listen closely. It's interesting to see if the poem changes when read out loud in their voice as sometimes they will put emphasis or a breath in a place that you didn't when you read it yourself. Hearing the poem read out loud by its author will sometimes give clues about the poet's intention for the poem which may not be clear from the text as it is on the page. Now it's time for the poet to be quiet, for the group to talk, and for the poem to stand on its own. The poet must not say anything to help their poem, which can feel very frustrating, especially if you are new to this. Some groups set a timer, so everyone has a fair amount of time allotted to their poem.

How do you give poetry feedback?
The point of sharing work with the group is to gain feedback from an objective audience. For example: there may be an area

in the poem which is not clear to others, not so much about 'meaning', but an unfocused or cryptic part that doesn't make sense within the world of the poem. You as the writer have lots of inside knowledge because you know exactly what it is supposed to be doing – you may be too close to see what confuses your reader. The rest of the group will say 'huh?' (Or something more articulate.) And then you can look closely to find what the confusion is and start to think about clarifying things.

Effective workshopping requires trust, sensitivity, and objectivity. At the start of every feedback session, participants sign an invisible pact, which basically consists of good manners. This is a poetry feedback group, and it is each member's responsibility to create a supportive environment in which you can grow as writers and learn from each other.

It would be foolish to say that subjectivity does not come into the reading of poems – it's a rare reader who comes to something with a completely clean slate of a mind, or no history on this earth of any kind. It's important to consider what your triggers might be. If for example, somebody has written a poem which contains a dog and your dog has been missing for a fortnight this might sway your emotions and therefore, your reading. In instances like this, I think it's best to be open where you are coming from. We are all human beings after all.

Here are some things to remember while offering feedback:
1. You are workshopping the writing, not the writer. The writer has entrusted the work to walk on its own feet. If it doesn't make it across to your side of the table, then there is a problem with this particular piece of writing, not the writer. It's the group's job to help with this process.
2. All participants should be allowed to speak about the poem if they have something to say, be it expressing concerns, asking questions or words of praise.
3. The most useful analysis of the nuts and bolts of a poem is

thinking not about what it means, but how it means. That is, think in terms of poetic technique.

4. Less useful feedback is praise which doesn't then expand into content. If you like a poem – try to think why and articulate it. Is it something about the imagery or a particularly powerful metaphor? Does the language sing? The poet needs to know what they are doing right; what connects with their reader.

5. Another kind of feedback which won't be useful to the writer is a simple: 'I don't understand'. Why might this be? Perhaps there are lines or words that don't belong in this poem. Perhaps the poem uses words you need to look up (look the words up; we can't know every word, and how else do we build a vocabulary?!). Or maybe the metaphor is mixed. Learning to articulate what isn't working for you in a poem will make you an insightful reader and a stronger writer and editor of your own work. All this becomes more instinctive, the more you do it.

And now some things to remember while receiving feedback:

1. Don't speak until the end. You have inside knowledge on your poem which can be released when the group has finished talking about it. Then you can ask questions, or perhaps come up with solutions to any issues raised.

2. Your writing is something you have made – it is not you. Any criticism of your work should not be taken personally, if the rest of the group is observing good manners.

3. Listen to what everyone says, and then make your own mind up. Differing opinions can be confusing, especially if you are a new writer. But if enough people have problems with the same part or aspect of your piece, then they are most probably right.

Is that everything, Helen?

Just a few more words of evangelism for the poetry feedback group. Showing work to my own group has become an important part of my writing process and they have seen drafts of many of the poems from all of my books. I become submerged in what I am doing, and I usually think of books as projects or bodies of work. My most recent two Bloodaxe books (*The Anatomical Venus, Constructing a Witch*) have been largely research-based. I have done so much historical and cultural research that sometimes I need the group to tell me if the poem works on its own, without all of the information in the reader's head. Going back to my creaturely metaphor at the start of this piece, it is often the case that my creatures are walking on their own, but after a nudge from my group, I am able to ensure they are walking in the direction I intended for them to go in, for the sake of the project.

Because we have been meeting as a group for a long time, we know what each other is working on and are able to bring a certain amount of familiarity to our critical reading. When helping people with their poems, it's well to remember that we are there to support the other poets to write like themselves, and not like us. In a workshop group, after a while, group members will probably be able to recognise the writing of other group members at a blind reading.

Not everybody will be content with the first group they join; many people move from one to another until they find somewhere they belong. Some will be members of more than one group and glean different things from the many different readers. I hope that this has been useful. I hope that you form, or find the right poetry feedback group/s for you.

ACTIVITY

This is an exercise in letting off steam in an unexpected direction. It is also an attempt to shake off your usual writing voice, which can sometimes feel like a habit that needs breaking, the more you write.

So, let's do something exaggerated to shake us up a bit. Write an angry poem about the sea, about a bus ticket, about some unsuspecting snail or a paperclip. Pick on something and corner it – address it in the first person if you want to get intimate.

Be irrational and imaginative – the more dramatic and passionate the better. Your focus may begin with the snail but can mushroom into aspects of snail-ness and everything that sails in it.

Spend twenty minutes writing without thinking to start with and then read back, see what you have begun; what might be developed. Most of all, have fun with it. Sometimes we forget to play. Play sets us free.

Clare Shaw

Working with Vulnerability in Groups

All poems must carry a Government warning. Words
Can seriously affect your heart.
(Elma Mitchell)

Introduction

Spoiler alert: there's no blueprint in this chapter. There's no universal definition of vulnerability, and no template for groupwork. You may finish with more questions than you started with.

But if you also take away a deeper appreciation of the ways that we make ourselves beautifully vulnerable in poetry, in groups and in connection – of the need for safeguarding and structure in groupwork – if you get to the end of this chapter asking questions about your own potential roles and responsibilities as a writer and a teacher or facilitator, and the gaps in your knowledge and skills – then that's good enough for me.

About me

Before I became a full-time writer, I made my living as a mental health trainer. And before that, I was a mental health service user. Rather than delivering mental health courses, these days I facilitate writing workshops. But I still work in psychiatric wards, community services and other places which can feel a million miles from the world of literature, along with the more predictable settings like universities, poetry festivals and writing centres. Because I know how transformative creative writing can be, I want as many people as possible to experience it – especially people who are distressed, or silenced or afraid.

Vulnerable and invulnerable groups

When I was first invited to write a chapter on 'Working with Vulnerable Groups', I thought back over the courses I've delivered recently – a six-week online course for survivors of childhood sexual abuse, for example, which was accompanied by a series of two-hour in-person workshops, and I thought about the enormous resilience I encountered in those groups. Then I considered two writing residentials I've recently delivered, and reflected on the very different emotional challenges they presented. And it occurred to me how the term 'vulnerable groups' creates a fake binary; how it implies that some people are inherently vulnerable whilst others are invulnerable. How it defines groups by their deficits rather than strengths, how it can function as a euphemism for 'problematic'.

That's why I chose instead to name this chapter 'Working with Vulnerability in Groups'. Because – although the legal definition of vulnerability is anyone who *needs special care, support, or protection because of age, disability, or risk of abuse or neglect* – in reality, vulnerability is a universal human experience. Because, when we acknowledge and work with vulnerability with transparency, courage and responsibility, it can be a resource, rather than a problem to be managed.

This chapter is aimed at anyone who works within writing, but it's especially intended as a provocation, if not a guide, for teachers, lecturers, workshop facilitators, festival organisers, and other writing group leaders. And it's based on the assumption that as group leader, you're not just there to teach people how to write. Your role also includes **making sure that each person is included**, heard and valued; and that the creative space is protected.

With this in mind, I've scattered a series of questions throughout this chapter, and I invite you to consider – what would *you do*? You might want to structure your response around these prompts:

- Whose responsibility is it to handle this situation?
- Is there any legislation or policy which may be relevant?

- How might this situation impact on you and what support might you need?
- Where can you access advice, support, and further resources?
- Was pre-emptive action needed? What action could you take to avoid this situation happening again?

Poetry is a lion

As Anna Severwright says, "If I put you in a room with a lion, you would be vulnerable." In many ways, poetry is that lion. It demands that we dip deeply into the well of ourselves. In our attempts to make sense of the world, we may find ourselves engaging with difficult experiences, thoughts and feelings. The essential mechanics of poetry – its use of metaphor and association, for example – invite us to connect with external and internal worlds intensely and to draw from our deepest places: particular techniques, like free writing, encourage us to bypass our own censors and inhibitions; particular forms, like the sonnets, provoke us to question and challenge ourselves, and return to our old truths in new ways. This can be a place of great joy, or humour. It can also be a place of pain.

– A group member starts crying as he shares his poem
– A 14 year-old participant reads out a poem describing self-injury

Writing in a group can be a particularly vulnerable experience – not just because every time we share a space with another human, we open ourselves to risk and possibility – but also because we tend to push ourselves harder in a group. It's easier to step beyond the boundaries of our comfort and safety, and into new territories where we may learn and grow – or conversely, we may feel overwhelmed and exposed.

Comfort and safety

Our experience of a group can be decided within minutes of arrival. A clean, pleasant venue and a greeting; a friendly, professional facilitator; a warm welcome from the group; a cup of tea – first impressions may tell us that this is somewhere we're going to feel accepted, where our needs will be met, our differences and limits recognised. Or – a dirty room, an unfriendly receptionist, a late-arriving, flustered workshop leader – our first minutes in a writing group may leave us feeling that our needs are going to be ignored, and our emotional safety neglected.

In reality, our experiences are shaped long before we enter a group. Although legislation and organisational structures and procedures are beyond the scope of this chapter, as a group leader or facilitator you should have considered all of these before your group arrives:

- Are you aware of any relevant legislation, policies and guidelines?
- Do you have a good understanding of diversity?
- Are you aware of access and learning needs within the group?
- Do you feel adequately skilled and resourced?
- Have you planned your workshop well?
- How can you access support and supervision?
- Have group participants received clear and helpful information about the group?
- Are you meeting at a suitable, safe time and place?
- Is the room comfortable? Can you alter the light and heating if necessary?
- Do people have access to refreshments/drinking water?
- Are you and the room ready for the group when they enter?

Transparency

We've established that, in writing groups, everyone is vulnerable sometimes. Are some people more vulnerable than others? Of course! If you're working with survivors of trauma or domestic violence, you might reasonably expect higher levels of anxiety and potential sensitivity to upsetting material.

– A group member is reading a lengthy piece about his experience of bereavement just before the end of the group
– A woman becomes tearful when her poem is critiqued in a feedback session

But vulnerability is filled with paradoxes. In the survivor groups I facilitated, many participants gave voice to painful memories and feelings, and sometimes there were tears. But the groups were also filled with determination, joy, empathy and kindness. Women drew on coping strategies they had developed over years; vulnerability was worn transparently and constructively, and multiple structures of support were in place to hold it. In contrast, although the writing residentials were not aimed at people with traumatic histories, in one group, a participant experienced a dramatic mental health crisis, and in another, conflict between group members caused distress for facilitators and participants alike.

Structure, structure, structure

Whatever the demographic or focus of your group, it is vital that participants know what to expect, and what is expected of them. Ground rules can play an important role in creating a sense of safety – but only if they truly reflect the needs and concerns of the group.

– A D/deaf group member is routinely excluded from other participants' discussions and socialising during a residential
– A student has a seizure during a lecture

At the beginning of the six-week course for survivors, we spent 30 minutes arriving at a group agreement – a detailed, collectively-agreed set of ground-rules. We began each session by reading this through, and we changed it when necessary. It can be easy to race through ground rules, assuming that everyone wants the same – punctuality, confidentiality, mobile phones off – but it's vital to remember that everyone's needs are different. For this reason, ground rules should be specific and concrete – for example, rather than just stating 'confidentiality', the group should be enabled to explain what they would like this to mean in practice – like, "Don't share personal stories outside of this group."

– *A participant with ADHD repeatedly interrupts and talks over other group members*
– *A man becomes tearful when his poem is critiqued by the group*

When we don't make our ground rules specific, they often rely on assumptions which usually reflect the attitudes and thoughts of the dominant cultural group – for example, the expectation that audiences should be silent during readings reflects a white, middle-class, 2023 version of Englishness. Similarly, 'trigger warnings' often reflect mainstream assumptions about what is normal and what is 'other': the survivor group described how poetry around abuse and assault could leave them feeling validated and heard, whereas poetry around happy, carefree childhoods could trigger feelings of grief and isolation.

Creating an open and inclusive discussion about needs also means that group members are more likely to work within ground rules and accept that sometimes they need to be enforced. This is a crucial responsibility of the facilitator – as is keeping to time. A clear schedule also lets us know what is going to happen, how, and when. Start and finish times – along with breaks and lunchtimes – are especially important, not just because they are about physical wellbeing and other practical considerations, but also because they mark the outer edges of the group. However fascinating the discussion, allowing the group to overrun can lead to a loss of trust in your ability to lead – and hold – the group.

– *One group member is upset and offended by swearing; another group member feels that it is an important part of her self-expression and culture*
– *A group member reads out a sexually explicit poem*

Taking your own needs seriously

But it's not all up to you. You are running this group as a writer, not a therapist. Your role has limits, as do you. You, like the participants, are a vulnerable human being. Whether you are self-employed or employed, you should have:

- A reasonable workload, with time to rest, recharge and be creative!
- Clarity about your role and clear boundaries around your work.
- Support with clarifying what your access needs are.
- Reasonable adjustments made to your work practice to reflect your access needs.
- Training and information so that you are informed and confident.
- Opportunities to talk and debrief with a valued colleague or peer.
- Access to emotional support when you need it.
- Back up from policies and guidelines, colleagues, managers and contractors.
- Recognition and acknowledgement of the work you're doing.
- Self-care, in whatever form you prefer!

Running groups is demanding work. If you are not recognising and responding to your own needs and vulnerabilities, your practice will suffer. And even more importantly, you may come to harm.

– You feel tired and ill three days into a challenging week-long residential
– During a tutorial, a student tells you they are in love with you

Conclusion

> *If a poem hasn't ripped apart your soul;*
> *you haven't experienced poetry.*
> (Edgar Allan Poe)

When I discussed this chapter with my friend, he showed me – with obvious disdain – this quotation, which has been doing the rounds on social media since it was first tweeted in 2014 by

147

@Edgar_Allan_Poe. As the author died in 1849, he is not likely to be tweeting – nor would he misuse a semi-colon. Disdain aside, the quote reflects a serious misconception: that poetry must be a shattering experience, and that in order to be a poet, you must suffer.

Not so. Writing a good poem is writing into life, and light. However difficult or joyful the topic, the poem must have a point of energy; however complex or simple the form, a good poem must be alive. Good poetry – like good group work, or good teaching – is sometimes hard. It takes us into dark places, into fear and trauma and grief. But it is also funny and fascinating, life-affirming and loving, utterly joyful. It is all of these things because we are knowingly, deliberately, carefully vulnerable. As Selima Hill says, "All poetry is love poetry." Because we recognise what is human and hurt in all of us, and because we respond with empathy, feeling and care.

Working with vulnerability in writing – and in groups – is not a matter of leaping in. It's treading deliberately, with skill and precision, with knowledge, using form and structure and technique. Delighting in the joy of language, and in humans connecting with each other. Delighting in communication, in care. Enjoy yourselves. Nobody needs to get hurt.

ACTIVITY

Writer and activist Anna Severwright argues that vulnerability is contextual, pointing out that, "If I put you in a room with a lion, you would be vulnerable." In another context, I would be thrilled, awestruck, profoundly moved. And also – potentially – dead.

Anna is critiquing the government's use of the term 'vulnerable groups'. But we are talking about poetry. Tell me about poetry as a wild animal. Tell me about that animal in your house. Tell me what it moves like, smells like, feels like. Tell me what impact it has on you – the joy it might bring you, or what harm you could come to in its presence.

Now repeat that exercise, but this time encounter the poem animal in a different setting. After several minutes of free writing, allow yourself, if you want, to stray out of the metaphor and talk more directly about vulnerability in writing.

Now read over what you've written … What have you learnt? What does this tell you about how you need to take care of yourself as a writer? Can you apply this same approach to the group?

Works Cited:

'Group Agreements for workshops and meetings' accessed at https://www.seedsforchange.org.uk/groupagree

Mitchell, E. (1987) *People Etcetera*, Peterloo Poets UK.

'Relaxed Venue' accessed at https://bac.org.uk/relaxed-venue/

Severwright, A. (2021) 'We are so much more', Community Catalysts https://www.communitycatalysts.co.uk/2021/03/18/we-are-so-much-more/ accessed 21st May 2023.

Whyte, D. (2019*) Consolations: The Solace, Nourishment and Underlying Meaning of Everyday Words* (Canongate, 2019).

Pat Edwards

Creating your own 'Poetry Community': Giving Back, Taking Part, Reviewing, Reading, and Making Space for Others

You don't need me to tell you that there are poetry people gathering to read, write, listen and share in the back rooms of pubs, in places of learning, arts venues, hubs and halls up and down the country. They do this with varying degrees of structure, funding and purpose. Sometimes there might be an organisation behind their efforts, offering guidance and ethos, but mostly it's down to the leadership and enterprise of individuals with simple aims and expectations. Nothing much of any worth happens in life without someone being prepared to give their time and energy to bring an idea to fruition, and that person could be you.

Making – taking part

> The fact of the matter is that the most unexpected and miraculous thing in my life was the arrival in it of poetry itself.
> (Seamus Heaney)

I first went to an organised poetry event about nine years ago. It was an open mic and I took along two poems I'd written, with the half-hearted intention of maybe reading them. I was pretty nervous but the room was small, and it seemed safe and welcoming enough, so I went ahead. I was in the middle of a course of chemo and it just felt so life-affirming and energising to share my work, however unpolished and imperfect it was. I had found my 'community'.

I started going to nights in Wrexham, Chester, Ludlow, Shrewsbury, Whitchurch ... anywhere I could find an open mic.

The breadth of different ages, styles, set-ups was as wide as there are genres of poetry and diversity amongst poets. It was a revelation. Wrexham was especially interesting, a night run by young poets in their early twenties who had managed to get the use of what had been a sports shop on the first floor of a town centre location. It was full of old sofas, the walls covered in modern artwork; it had a make-shift bar run by volunteers, and offered sarnies, crisps and biscuits in the interval. The welcome was second to none, every poet called to the stage with 'let's hear it for …' or 'make some noise', like we were superstars on the circuit. I was much older than most of the poets there, but no one cared, we were all equal, valid, valued for our contribution. What an experience, to read poetry to an engaged, expectant audience, and to be cheered and clapped no matter what. I really learned about presentation, using a mic, how to project and connect. I'll be forever grateful to the team and set-up at Voicebox.

Doing – giving back

Wanting something literally closer to home, I sought to set up my own open mic night, and found a local bistro with a back room barely used except for storing chairs and boxes. The owner was more than happy for me to tart up the space with a few lights, flowers and a banner, and Verbatim was born. Not withstanding the hiatus caused by Covid, Verbatim survived as an in-person event.

I have this 'thing' I do in response to every single open mic poet at Verbatim; I try to say something, no matter how small, about their reading. Poets rarely get feedback for their work, beyond a murmur, a round of polite applause, perhaps a kind word from someone during the interval. I might repeat back to them a phrase I've enjoyed or concur on an opinion expressed. Maybe I'll comment on their successful use of repetition or alliteration, or on a striking image. I'm sure I don't always get it right but I try, and I think poets appreciate that I've listened and taken the trouble.

When a poet reads their piece aloud to an audience at an open mic, it is often the first time the poem has been heard. They get one chance to take in the details, the way the poet has structured things, used words to create music, meaning, atmosphere, if indeed they have. Sometimes the images rush passed so quickly, confusing the ear, mesmerising the listener. To be a good listener is hard, demands concentration, effort, engagement. I've been to open mics where people have been on their phones, clearly busy getting their own poems organised ready to read, or are even whispering to their companion. Being a listener is an act of commitment, where you make a contract with the poets, promising to give them your full attention in exchange for their most precious thoughts and ideas. The poet has a responsibility too, has to have their audience in mind, choose work wisely. No wonder us poets have got to do our best to pay attention to detail and to hone our craft. If readers and listeners are going to scrutinise our efforts, we better hit them between the eyes with some bangers!

What does it take to organise a poetry night? These days, you don't even need a venue; you just need an account with an online platform. You need to know what format you're going to present: guest reader, theme, selected collection, discussion, reading, open mic, Q&A – or something hybrid? If you do go down the in-person route, the venue does become important, because cost, availability, location, acoustics, etc. will all play a part. A free room at the back of a pub may sound attractive but not if there are going to be major distractions like the jukebox next door or fans screaming at the large-screen TV when the big game is on. You want a bit of atmosphere and comfort if at all possible. You can do simple things to create this with a banner, flowers, cushions, screens, a decent mic if it's a big space, maybe refreshments, that sort of thing. In the end, it does come down to having the confidence to stand up and say stuff! You need a compère who will act as 'master of ceremonies', keep order, direct proceedings, build rapport, be a bit bossy, and leave their ego at home.

I know admin is boring but I'd recommend a few simple things just to protect yourself, and to help chart your progress and development as an event. Keep records, and do it at the time, not weeks after the gig when you've forgotten details or lost receipts. Do your admin in a little notebook or on a spreadsheet, whatever works for you, just as long as you can share it with others if you're asked to. The sort of things to record might include: date, how much you spent on the venue, refreshments, guest poet, what you took on the door and how many people attended. Even if you only give your guest poet a tenner towards their travel, that could be £100 or more over the course of a year. Likewise, if ten people give you £3 entry every time, that could be in excess of £300 cash that is not yours, but effectively belongs to your event. Personally, I opened a bank account because just having a 'petty cash' system felt a bit too loose. Besides, you can't apply for grants unless you've got an account into which these can be deposited.

When it comes to something such as a poetry festival, this is an altogether bigger affair. The kind of income and expenditure you will be managing will require someone with accountancy skills to keep proper records. It's good to have trusted individuals around you to help share the responsibilities, even if this amounts to a very small committee and a few volunteers. To apply for funding you will need a constitution, policies around areas such as data storage, health and safety, safeguarding, equal opportunity. You need to do your research, take advice from people who have proven experience and dip your toes in the water carefully at first. You can still be ambitious – please be ambitious! – but don't expect overnight success, and be prepared for disappointment, especially on the funding front.

These days there is, quite rightly in my opinion, a greater commitment to accessibility. If the Covid crisis taught us anything, it taught us that online experiences are a valid way of providing access for people who cannot, for a multitude of reasons, attend in-person events. This means that organisers should consider ways of incorporating at least some access via online platforms. I am personally committed to doing what I can, with the resources I can muster, to improve accessibility. Remember, if applying for funding from organisations such as Arts Council England or Arts Council Wales, for instance, you can include some funds specifically to cover the costs of making your event more accessible as part of your overall funding budget. However, in my own experience, it has not always been a 'given' that funding will magically come your way just because you have this admirable aim. Even if only part of what you can provide is available online or in hybrid format, this is progress and a move in the right direction. Another important thing I would like to emphasise is to get the technical stuff as good as you can afford to make it. Some will tell you it's easy to learn and to upskill yourself. In my experience, seek out the professionals who know their fields. You can't be expected to be a master of everything.

Make good friends in all aspects of running a festival. Nice people exist. Generous people exist. People who don't want to rip you off exist. Talk to them. Be cheeky, no – not cheeky, just honest, and tell them upfront what you can afford to pay them. They can walk away disgruntled and insulted if they want to; maybe they're not the right people for you. We all have our price, fair enough, but things find their 'level' and you have to balance what feels equitable and in the best interest of your event and its values, and manage expectations. If this sounds hard, it is believe me, but don't let it put you off.

Perhaps the hardest thing about any of this is having belief and confidence. Maybe you have wanted to organise something for ages. I used to lie in bed at night, or get distracted at work, dreaming and plotting. I would get carried away with thoughts of banners all over town, TV and radio running features, hundreds of people flocking to the festival to end all festivals.

Dreams are fun, but my reality came down to one day a year in June, in a church hall, on a wing and a prayer, with some lovely people, doing what we treasure. A friend of the festival once described it as "punching above its weight", and that pretty much sums it up. We've had some of the most respected contemporary poets grace our stage over the years, because they shared our aspirations and wanted to bring poetry to a place they knew it would be truly appreciated. It's not always about big venues, large audiences and selling merchandise; it's about integrity, authenticity and a kind of purity of intention. Dream big, grasp reality, and just do it. It's a bit like writing a poem: you have an idea, something you think needs saying; you start to write a few words and phrases; you edit; you put it away then go back to it again and again; you make a decision that it's the best it can be in this moment, at this time; you press 'send' and it's out in the world. One day you get your first acceptance, your first publication. So, why not ask a few friends to your place to share and talk about poetry? Why not find a public venue, do the same, only a bit more organised? Why not have a little more ambition for what you've started? Why not get a bit of help, seek a sponsor, find some funding, grow? Why not be a 'doer'?

Reading, reviewing, leading workshops

If you're going to hire poets to read at your events, you need to know what poets are writing about and how they're doing it – read! If you're going to take up writing yourself and want to work on your craft – read! If you're going to run workshops – read! Something I love to do is to close-read a pamphlet or collection, to try to get under the skin of the writer, and to sum up my thoughts in a review. It's not about having an opinion and thinking everyone needs to hear it. I prefer the idea that you're giving other readers a bit of a helping hand, a heads-up on what they might get out of the work. Of course, everyone has their own take on poetry and they may get something totally different out of the pieces, but it's fun to share, debate, consider.

Importantly, I think poets appreciate someone taking the time to read their new work and they surely find it interesting to know how things came across, penetrated, evoked emotions.

Another favourite thing – I'm spoilt for choice when it comes to all things 'poetry' – is to research and lead workshops, usually around a theme. I have just the best of times thinking up topics, finding exemplar poems, creating prompts and putting together resource packs. To see heads down, pencils scratching, poems gestating amongst my loyal workshoppers, is a total joy. And then, when they read their poems at an open mic or share them with me for a bit of extra feedback, it's a genuine privilege to have played a small part in bringing their poems to life. Better still if they go on to get something published.

This poetry lark; we're all in it together. That's what a community is, a unit with a common purpose. Let's take part, give back, get involved in an artistic wave that needs us as doers, makers, writers, readers and listeners.

> The blood jet is poetry and there is no stopping it
> (Sylvia Plath)

ACTIVITY

I'm thinking about that open mic where everyone was introduced with 'let's hear it for ...' or 'make some noise for ...' It made the poets feel important and welcome.

Use either or both of those phrases as a refrain or repeated chant in your poem. Base the poem on people or things you feel deserve a 'shout out', are worthy of our respect and love. Maybe go for the unsung, the ordinary, the ignored. Of course, you can go off on any tangent that comes to you, and use imagery and other poetic devices that take your fancy. For example:

Let's hear it for the dinner ladies, the bin men, the road sweepers who get their hands dirty and make our hearts gleam.

Make some noise for the dog walkers, the fence painters, the garden makers who stride, swish and shovel through seasons and cigarettes.

Finish on a flourish, something like –

Blessed are the open mic-ers for they shall inherit applause!

Jonathan Davidson

Funding Your Plans

The first funder of the arts is always the artist, and so it is with poetry. At various and most times in our writing lives, if we want to make something we must give our time freely and quite possibly spend a bit of money. Thankfully, poetry demands little specialist equipment other than inordinate talent and the greater talent, which is to apply it. Some notepads, a fistful of pencils (plus sharpener) and perhaps a cheap laptop won't set one back terribly much. And the books by other poets – vital for development – can be borrowed from libraries or friends. However, there comes a time when some funds might be of use, mainly in buying time, of which we all have only a limited supply, although in this essay I'll also look at other costs that might be covered by a third party.

To be funded one needs to have a plan. This can be as simple as 'finish enough poems to make a pamphlet', although if a plan is too 'everyday' (with respect to those assembling pamphlets) it does make finding funds more difficult. Still, writing poems is often at the heart of a 'poetry plan', and that's no bad thing. Funders will sometimes simply fund the time to sit (or stand or walk or run) to do this, so long as they feel this activity will give them what they want. And here I arrive at the first truth that must be acknowledged, which is that although funders claim that they primarily serve the art or the artist, in order to do this they must also be greatly concerned for their own objectives and targets.

So having only lightly touched upon the 'plan', let's think a bit more about the funder. Funders – and funding – come in two broad categories: public funding and private funding. Public funding, in the home nations of the UK certainly, tends to be distributed either directly by a tax-raising body, typically a local authority or national government, or via some arm's-length body, i.e. one that has funding from taxation but distributes it with a degree of independence. Arts Council England (ACE) receives some of its millions from His Majesty's Government, via the Treasury, although most funding from ACE for smaller projects will come from private sources, see below. I'll be mentioning ACE quite a bit in this article, but my experience is that funders from the other home nations (and possibly beyond) have a similar approach to funding. So, if you are not in England please do read all about Arts Council England and then refer to the websites of your country's arts funding body for their particular details.

Private funding can come from anything between an individual citizen putting some money in a hat to a grant-giving trust or foundation – often a registered charity – dispersing funds that may have been accrued over many centuries of 'wise' investment (which might include unsavoury sources, let us be honest). Private funding can also come from businesses, keen to align themselves with art or artists, or the communities served by the same. Again, real though their money is, some of it is 'dirty'. Wherever the money comes from, from taxation or from profits or from returns on investment or from the charitable inclination of a single citizen, it pays to think a little about what is wanted in return.

The rather unorthodox advice I find myself constantly giving to others is to use one's powers of imagination and creativity to 'empathise' with the funder. You have your plan – yes, we'll come back to that soon – but they have their plan, which is to use their money to make happen the things they want to make happen. It might be the warm feeling of satisfaction that comes from a modest personal donation, or it might be to benefit a community negatively impacted by a business, or it might be to deliver the aims and objectives offered by a local authority or government department. ACE are perfectly and delightfully clear about this. They need the things and/or the people they fund to contribute to ACE's objectives (their Outcomes) and to use ACE's 'Investment Principles' to achieve those Outcomes.

At this point, the poet with a poetry plan could be forgiven for feeling rather inadequate. Poetry rarely spends money on mighty citadels of culture through which secondary income can be generated by the sale of ice creams during intervals. And although poetry can make much happen and is generally a positive experience (at least for those writing/speaking it), it also, to use Auden's phrase out of context, 'makes nothing happen'. Well, this is where we must be creative. We must shape a plan so that it might beyond all reasonable doubt be considered capable of delivering some quantity of whatever 'return' the funder demands.

As a little case study, let's look at ACE's Developing Your Creative Practice fund, a fund not dissimilar to other schemes in the home nations and beyond. The words tattooed on the knuckles of this fund should be taken to heart. In this instance, ACE want YOU to DEVELOP, and what they want you to develop is YOUR PRACTICE, i.e. how you work as an artist. This is a great start and to continue, the wise poet would certainly make haste to ACE's website by searching for ACE DYCP to find pages of fine detail. But let us pause for a moment to ask the obvious question: why?

Well, in this instance, ACE will suggest that the health and welfare of culture generally is reliant on artists of all forms being active. And not only must they be active, but they must also develop, which is code for 'go from being possibly good and interesting to probably very good and very interesting'. You as a poet may sit somewhere along this spectrum. In addition, ACE has identified that many people do not engage (i.e. participate, attend, consume) arts and culture as much as do others, and given that most people pay for it, that ain't right. So if you are in or from such a category – perhaps you are not to the cultural manor born – then ACE will be particularly interested in helping you develop.

I digress for a moment to note that much of ACE's small-scale funding comes from the National Lottery, a government-sanctioned, regulated and encouraged gambling opportunity. So, indirectly this money is from many millions of regular folk who buy a scratch card or choose some numbers to brighten up their evening. Given the source of this funding – which is many people from just about everywhere – it might well be that ACE is particularly concerned that this funding as far as possible heads back to 'many artists' from 'just about everywhere', including poets. Keep that in mind.

But back to the DYCP fund. In the plan – the poetry plan – the poet will need to have need for some form of 'development' which will improve the poet's 'artistic practice'. ACE is slightly less enthusiastic about this being just another collection or even a first collection – possibly because if they funded such things easily the demand released would swamp them – but ACE is enthusiastic about working with mentors or with communities or with places, all to make the poet an artist who has 'developed'. So, to develop by switching from prose to poetry or switching from short-form poetry to long-form poetry, or from being a page poet to a performance poet, all these are fundable developments.

We are starting to shape some plans here. And in the case of DYCP, so long as the plan develops an artist (that's you, dear poet) and is more than just more of the same, then it is 'in with a shout', as I believe professional fundraisers say. I use the very formal phrase 'in with a shout' when what I should say is that this fund – and most others – are competitive and to simply reach the criteria for being fundable does not mean funds will come forth. Far more people apply than can be satisfied, so many are disappointed. Their work is fundable, but ACE, or whoever it is, simply didn't have enough money at the time of application to fund everyone. My advice is to take this as you would take all rejection: with stoicism and privately. Resist the temptation to display the bareness of your disappointment publicly, or direct it towards Arts Council England or any other funding body concerned. But do read the feedback, if any has been given, and do ask advice from others who have been in a similar position before.

Funders, including ACE and local authorities and bodies funded by other governments, typically have other funds which, while not directed at you as an artist, might allow you to be funded to do what you want so long as some other people benefit. The classic plan is the 'poet in residence' or 'poetry engagement programme' (workshops, readings, etc.), which give the funders what they want by giving benefits to 'communities'. A community can be absolutely anything you want it to be, so long as more than one person is involved. It could be a housing estate whose elders would benefit from reading poetry aloud together, or it could be people who have the same life experience and would do well to write about it, or it could be those who happen to be visitors to a particular museum and who didn't know how much they would enjoy reading poems about paintings.

The trick, of course, is to describe your plan in such a way that the funder can see it is also what they want to happen to achieve their stated aims. And beyond that, the trick is to construct a plan that does the above while also allowing one to be artistically fulfilled and financially remunerated. If you don't like museums don't plan a poetry project in one, obviously. But who doesn't like a museum? I've mentioned money there, and this is a good time to say that funders are happy for the starving artist to have enough cash to buy the occasional bag of chips with optional vegan saveloy. They know the poet's time is money and, just as they don't work as well-paid managers of grant-giving funds for nothing, so they don't expect artists to live on thin air.

The principles, if they can be given that grand title, being laid out here are perhaps overly simple. Understand what your funder might want from you and try to give them that. Looking at the slightly bigger picture, one might suggest that this notion of those with money giving it to activities that at first sight appear to be more circus-focused than bread-focused is a post-WWII concept, widely supported across the western world and that this consensus is still just about in place. Well, it is just that. And it would do well for us to remember that when a poetry project is funded, it is because, somewhere along the line, those with the money thought this would accrue a range of benefits. Many of these benefits will be difficult to measure, uncertain in their realisation and quite possibly not as good as hoped. But such is, let's face it, life itself, so three cheers for the post-war consensus on the funding of cultural engagement from public and private funds for the greater good or some, if not all, of the nation's citizens, say I.

In previous millennia, art and culture was also funded, although it was a likely to be at the gift of the rich and powerful and possibly for their aggrandisement (*plus ça bleedin' change,* I hear you say). Unless they just made their own art/fun, the individual had little input, so perhaps we are not so different. Well, there has been one big change in funding, and that is the use of the internet – I don't know if you have heard of the internet, it is jolly good – to secure funding from many individuals to enable an arts activity to happen before there is anything to sell. In poetry, this takes the form of the 'crowdfunded' publication, which is brilliant because not only does it put some money in the bank to pay the creatives (poets, designers, etc.) but it demonstrates that there is actual interest in the project. There's a novelty, knowing some people who want it before you go to the bother of making it!

And the beauty of crowdfunding – or we might call it subscribing, which reveals its roots in how the upper and middle classes of the Enlightenment funded their culture – is that the individual poet can drive the process, relying on their networks and the value, in the minds of the many right-thinking individuals, of their work. And if this funding is seen as 'matching funding', i.e. some resource to put alongside funding from a more regular funder, it can actually help to lever out funds by demonstrating to the funder that there is interest (and some additional cash). The principle, of course, is the same, in that the poet needs to persuade the citizens that what they want is the happiness that will be engendered by the poems/the book/the project. Again, empathise with those who have the money to help them see their way to giving you some of it.

I draw this canter through the lush fields of funding to a close by offering a few final notes. Find out about your funder, empathise with your funder and try to make what you want to do fit in with what they want to fund. Accept that the process of applying needs thoughtful preparation and will take weeks or months. No outcome is certain, but a careful approach improves one's chances. See yourself and your work as an example of high-quality art either getting better or being experienced by more people, even if the engagement of others might be quite a long time in the future. Learn from others by asking how they got their funding; better still read other people's successful applications (with their permission, of course). Finally, use the process of shaping an application to help you develop clarity in your own plans. When ACE ask you what you are going to do and how are you going to do it, they not only want to know themselves but they want you to have been through that thought process. In this respect, even an application that might fail can offer some value. Oh, and if you fail first time around, apply again. They had probably run out of money, and they might not run out next time.

ACTIVITY

To get ready for any funding application, using bullet points, list your story so far: what you have done, who has supported you, for instance through publication.

Then, also with bullet points, list the elements of your plan. If it doesn't neatly bullet-point, it isn't a plan.

Then, finally, using more from your infinite supply of bullet points, list the short, medium, and long-term positive outcomes of your being funded, both for you directly and for the rest of the known world.

Use your imagination, be a little bit over the top, dream a happy dream.

Having done this, you are ready to begin your funding application.

Part Three

Projects in Public

Julia Bird

Learning to Loom: Producing, Staging and Touring Poetry Shows

There's an overheard quote recorded in the tour diary I kept for one of the live literature shows I've produced: it's one theatre techie talking to another during the get-in. "John, I'm just looming up now!" I wrote it down because I wasn't exactly sure I knew what it meant – something to do with a sudden surprising appearance maybe, something to do with weaving? What poet isn't intrigued by an incongruous, ambivalent eavesdrop? I checked the word's definition. During the get-in, that period when stage, lighting and sound is prepared for a forthcoming theatrical performance, a *loom* refers to the tidy bundle of power and other cables that might run from a control desk to a lighting rig. I've always been comfortable around words and their shifting meanings. How to manage theatre technicians is a skill I've had to learn.

Jaybird Live Literature is the live lit production company I founded in 2006. It's a micro-organisation – while there are designers, directors and others I work with regularly, it's only me on the books permanently. Amongst the Jaybird projects I've run, I've produced eight touring live lit shows, each one funded on a project-by-project basis by Arts Council England. The shows have reached dozens of venues and thousands of audience members, touring down as far as Truro and up as far as St Andrews.

On my very direct journey from a bookish childhood to an Eng Lit degree, I didn't stop off at the theatre. I didn't study drama or join any extra-curricular clubs – but my first job out of university was in an arts centre that had a tiny pocket handkerchief stage. The weekly transformations made to that bare space by small touring theatre companies with no more props and costumes than could be transported in the back of a Volvo stayed with me. Later, as I started working professionally for literature organisations and writing my own poems, I went to many, many poetry readings – everywhere from 2,000 seater auditoria to tiny pub back rooms. I started to wonder if the production values I'd experienced with those touring theatre shows could be combined creatively with poetry. I never wanted distraction from the power of the words on the page or the air, but I wanted to know what would happen if I added lighting design, sound or direction to the familiar poet-and-a-standing-mic reading.

In the mid-noughties, there was money around to spend on the arts. Arts Council England actively called out for writers, arts admins and venues to experiment with the beginnings of this new art form that was coalescing under the banner 'live literature'. I remember sitting in those first briefing meetings with the people who would go on to form Adverse Camber and Penned in the Margins – and go on to actually *be* Luke Wright. Gratefully supported by cash and the time to experiment, I started to imagine how my own live literature shows might unfold.

An hour of poetry on stage at a literature festival or bookshop reading – that's easy enough to fill. Three poets each reading from their latest books for 15 minutes with a bit of patter, a cheery host to introduce all the writers' biographical details and an audience Q&A to finish. I wondered what would happen if you strip away all those expectations – no host, no inter-poem chat or explanations, and definitely no on-stage enquiries about how the clock is running down and if there's time for just one more poem. Just poems, read aloud. For ideas about how to fill a non-narrative hour on stage, I went to see lots of contemporary dance shows, and took notes about how lighting and sound underscore the intentions of the dancers, how patterns are made in time and space by alternating the speeds of sections of the performance. I don't have a dance background either – my notes probably just said something along the lines of *fast dancing / slow dancing / more fast dancing* – but I was beginning to understand how decisions about pace and scale of performance affect an audience's emotions. Dancers might begin and end a show with the same gestures in the same position on stage – but the second time you see those movements, your understanding is deepened by all that has happened in performance in the previous 45 minutes. You could read the same poem at the beginning and the end of a set for the same effect, I thought.

If I wanted to use complex lighting and sound, I had to make shows that would fit into spaces that had those technical facilities – i.e. fully equipped theatres, not literature festival tents or pub rooms. If I wanted theatres to buy in my shows, I had to make something that appealed directly to their potential audiences. Big poetry names will sell tickets to those already in the know, but not to those who aren't immersed in the world. I needed to make shows that were thematic, with a clear claim on an audience's attentions. Here is a show about *Love* or *Adolescence* or *Power*, I would tell theatre bookers. It will make your audiences feel embraced or included or enraged, I'd tell the marketing staff.

I started with the poets. Page poets, rather than spoken word artists – I'm one of the former, and that's the background I *do* claim with confidence. During those many, many poetry readings, I'd developed a sense of the writers who had an innate stage presence and who might be amenable to an invitation to present their work in unfamiliar ways. I wanted to cast groups of poets with a range of experiences whose interspersed poems would complement each other. *You Are Here* was the Jaybird show featuring Colette Bryce, Daljit Nagra and Jo Shapcott. Before we ever got near a rehearsal room, I spread loose poems from all of their books over my sitting room floor to look for the connections between them, the logic to determine how the poems would follow each other in a script. The poems that rose to the top of the pile under my gaze were all the ones written in the first person – I gathered about 45 of them, an hour's worth. All written in the I / me voice: aha, so this was going to become a show about *Identity*. The selected poems then began to group into categories – anecdotal, confessional, fantastical. The more I shuffled the pages, the more the poems with their various modes of address organised themselves like a progressively more intimate conversation. I imagined a party full of strangers, where the small talk starts polite then veers off. This then became the structure of the show: six sections of poems, each section corresponding to the stages of a party. The section titles are still handwritten all over my rehearsal notebooks – *Who Are You And What Do You Do / I'll Tell You A Story / I'll Tell You A Secret / Drunken Flights Of Fancy / It's My Party And I'll Cry If I Want To / Let's Stay In Touch* – each section filled with a related selection of the three poets' work. The show didn't look like a party – there were no balloons or party poppers visible to the audience – but its internal, secret party logic is what gave it a structure robust enough to stand up as a theatrical performance.

Confirming poets, poems, themes and order was as far as I could get on my own. To move the shows in my head out into the world, I needed to bulk up my micro-organisation with imported knowledge and skills. Before I made any shows, I was mentored by Penny Mayes who founded Trestle Theatre Company, one of the UK pioneers of touring mime theatre. She taught me how to sell shows into venues. The first show I made (*Tilting the Mirror* with Jean Sprackland, Greta Stoddart and the work of Ray Robinson) was a collaboration with Millfield Theatre in Edmonton. I needed to learn how to make work in a theatre space, and an establishment name would buttress my untested company identity when it came to marketing the show. I knew the Millfield's then artistic director was poetry friendly from working with him in a previous job, and was pleased he welcomed my invitation to co-produce. Above all, I needed a director to move the poets meaningfully on stage, and was very glad to reconnect with Phoebe Stout, a friend from home, who had just finished her drama school director's training.

Poems are not plays and poets are not actors: Phoebe and I knew that we never wanted to dramatise poetry or ask poets to learn lines, but we were interested to consider what theatrical techniques we might use to highlight the substance of the work. The rehearsal period to make each show we called 'drama school in a week' – we did lots of work with the poets on posture and breathing, and experimented with changing reading pitch, pace and volume. The shows had sets – a table and chairs for *You Are Here*, a mock-up of a YouTuber's bedroom for *What Days We're Having Now* (Ella Frears, Will Harris and Alex MacDonald. I handmade 200 faux Polaroids for that set). The poets moved around in a fixed choreography, depending on whether they were reading to each other, to the audience or to themselves. Alex and Ella held hands downstage to read poems to each other, Clare Pollard knelt in a pile of prop letters for one of her monologues in *Ovid's Heroines*. We made physical and visual images to speak to the images of the poems. John Castle, our lighting designer, focused and defined the audience's attention with his work, teaching me how to think visually while at the same time greatly increasing my productive technical vocabulary. 'Straw' and 'steel' are names for light – terms which have made their way into a number of my poems since.

With each show, we aimed to teach ourselves new skills. *What Are They Whispering?* (Imtiaz Dharker, Joe Dunthorne and John Stammers) was a show about power, with the secret structure of an election cycle. We wanted a very hard look to this show, which we achieved with a TV studio-style lighting design, lots of cut up static on the soundtrack, and a fake-exploding lighting rig. At the end of the show, Imtiaz pulled apart a rigged-up electrical coupling, which cued an explosion of fireworks and a total lighting black-out. 'Trained pyrotechnician' still sometimes turns up on my CV. For *The Retold Ramayana* – a second Jaybird booking for Daljit Nagra – we commissioned cartoon versions of the epic's characters, and just about mastered the controls of the massive projector needed to beam out the illustrations before the premiere performance.

Not all our discoveries were technical: *I Gaze From My Kitchen Like an Astronaut* was an acoustic show. We made twenty-minute mini-shows for ten poets (including John McCullough whose poem 'The Light of Venus' provided the overall show title). Venues booked the selection of poets to fit their requirements. Lots of props to manipulate here: Sarah Howe had a bunch of real tulips that represented in turn the paint brush, jewellery and lotus leaf imagery of her poems; Amy Key had an atomiser of vanilla perfume to create the show's personalised scentscape. We were booked for a haunted house, libraries, galleries, museums and supper-clubs on this tour, taking everything we'd learned about large-scale shows and miniaturising it.

Maxed-out or mini, the spirit of a Jaybird show is collaborative and exploratory – all shows to date have been made from a combination of many poets' and artists' ideas. They wouldn't have happened at all without Sarah Sanders and David Cross from Arts Council England, Phoebe Stout and John Castle: my heartfelt thanks goes to them. There are shows I still want to make but, as freelance production can be financially precarious, I am currently sheltering in the lee of a PAYE job. For future Jaybird developments or to get in touch meanwhile, check www.jaybird.org.uk

ACTIVITY: How to zhuzh up your poetry performance

Even the shortest poetry reading can benefit from some theatrical razzmatazz.

1. Google acting warm-up exercises for the body and voice, and adapt them to suit your circumstances. Prepare your lungs, lips and tongue to articulate your words.
2. Plan your set in sections. If you've got 20 minutes to read, you can fit in 2-3 mini sections. How do you move your audiences through varying moods? What happens if you read the same poem twice?
3. Play with the pitch, speed and volume of your reading voice – which poems need slowness and quiet, which speed and a fizzing energy?
4. Can you change position on stage? Hard if you're behind a standing mic, but can you move your head, hands or stance to add variety to the audience's perceptions?
5. What are you reading from? Papers which wobble and rattle? What if half your set is read from a black notebook, and half from a neon yellow one? What happens if you put aside your books and recite a poem from memory, or plant a friend in the audience to read one on your behalf?
6. Costume: what do we think?

Jo Bell

There's a Unicorn in the Staff Canteen! Being a Poet in Residence

Are you slightly mystified by what a poet in residence does? You are not alone. Even some of the organisations who employ them start from the same point.

What we usually mean by a residency is that a poet is embedded for a certain period in a place, an organisation, or an event, and paid to write about it. The residencies advertised on social media or in poetry journals will set you inside a cultural organisation – say Dartington Historic Gardens or the National Railway Museum – or inside a festival, a community group or corporation. You work with staff and volunteers; you engage with passers by, or synthesise what the company does into a poetic manifesto.

A residency is a form of public poetry. It's a way of working which can accelerate your writing career. It brings you new subjects and audiences, good things to put on your CV and a sensible fee. It disrupts your usual writing habits, forcing you to write quickly whilst disorientated by unfamiliar cultures. You may have to balance your creative integrity against the need for a poem about the composting toilets in the visitor centre.

The poet in residence is not literally resident. They will probably spend some time on site, making a behind-the-scenes tour at a museum, gathering stories from a youth group, or talking to travellers at a railway station. There's often an expectation of (and a contract for) certain outcomes, but very often, you have some leeway to shape them yourself. An art gallery would like poems for the café walls; a festival wants a roaming poet, visible and versatile. You might be asked to deliver workshops for school groups, or to perform at an end-of-project gig. It's a kind of outreach work. The host borrows the alchemy of poetry, to tap into a register of language that visitors will recognise as special. You begin to feel like a unicorn, bringing a glimpse of magic into the staff room.

Residency is both an income stream and an opportunity for personal development. As poets in the Western tradition, we are used to writing lyric poetry, i.e. writing about ourselves and (let's be honest) seeking praise. We are switched to 'transmit'. A poet in residence switches to 'receive', and works in the service of other voices. You are asked to ventriloquise the feelings of workers in some special place: gardeners, curators, hospital porters. That means listening to them in the first place.

Dan Simpson is the poet in residence at the National Memorial Arboretum. His experience gives an idea of the responsibility and surprise that can come out of a residency.

> The first thing I had to do was to write a poem for the dedication of the Glade, to frontline workers who lost their lives during Covid. My opening act was the Dean of Westminster, who I next saw crowning the King ... It's an honour to be in those spaces, and to give a poem.

I have felt this too. In a residency at a Women's Aid refuge, I assisted women in writing around (and away from) their experiences of abuse. Sometimes they cried, sometimes they roared with laughter. Always, they were invested in helping me to express what domestic violence does, on their behalf. They shared deep intimacies. The resulting poetry literally empowered them.

Any residency has three potential benefits:

Financial reward:	Actual put-it-in-the-bank money
Creative reward:	New subjects and locations, chances to develop as a writer, collaborations, creative challenges
Professional reward:	Profile, contacts, skill building, work that looks good on the CV

It is unlikely that you'll get all three at once, and the first two are often mutually exclusive, but there is always some creative opportunity. Whether the host is an institution like the RSPB or a corporation, you are making applied poetry, with a ready-made audience. Residency offers creative experiment and privileged human encounters. If you write something which pleases the organisation and also satisfies your writerly ambition, then you are in the sweet spot where financial reward meets meaningful art. So, the *creative* reward may be considerable.

Usually, the *professional* reward is valuable too. You develop a template for use in similar settings, or get a few lines of testimonial for your home page: you build skills in crowdsourcing and creating trust. Dan Simpson says:

> Most residencies are about engagement. You need good facilitation and space-holding skills. You need to be unflappable, and not seen as a threat.

All of this will serve you well in future work.

The residency at Women's Aid was one that I built myself, by approaching them and writing a joint application for a small grant. Financial reward: sufficient. Creative reward: moderate. Professional reward: significant, in terms of new skills and confidence. The relationship continued for several years. Personal reward: immense. We'll come back to these self-building residencies later.

Working around challenges is another professional gain. During a residency at a hospital, I knew that patient confidentiality was key – so my poems were full of fake patients, with fake names. The resulting work was still rejected as 'too realistic'. It *looked* as if the hospital was compromising patient privacy. I wrote new material and got a better understanding of the client's needs. Professional rewards all round, and a respectable fee.

By contrast, my residency at Glastonbury Festival earned a £50 fee [sic] plus festival entry and food vouchers. Financial reward:

actually negative since it didn't even pay for the petrol. Creative reward: negligible. Professional reward: significant. I wrote fast and on demand, raised my profile, got a good byline for the CV – and saw Stevie Wonder.

Grow your own

For most residencies, you write an application like any other job. They are few and far between, so keep an eye on the Facebook group *Literary Residencies: open calls for writers and translators*, and run a Google search every few weeks. Do not tell yourself that you aren't ready. Like parenthood, this is something you will only learn by doing it.

If the residency you want doesn't exist – then *build it yourself*. Create opportunities as well as poems. Carving out your own residency does so many good things for you. It fosters confidence as you identify a venue, make contacts, explore funding, explain how poetry can help an organisation.

As you go, you'll see how the three kinds of reward feed into one another. Tania Hershman's recent work shows how a self-built residency which at first offered only creative rewards, can bring professional and financial benefits too.

Case study: Tania Hershman

A former science journalist, Tania had already written a story collection inspired by a year's residency in a biochemistry lab. A few years later, moving to a flat near Manchester's Southern Cemetery, she was curious about the stories the cemetery might tell. Thanks to a local tour guide, she made contact with staff, who warmly welcomed her. Tania made her own timetable, met with gravediggers and took photos of gravestones. She searched for those of women who, like herself, weren't described as 'wife' or 'mother'.

With no constrictive brief, she was able to push her writing in new directions. Tania worked with the tour guide to build a new walking tour-plus-writing-workshop. Her writing project became part of a novel, Go On, later published by Broken Sleep.

By now her cemetery residency was attracting attention, and she was commissioned to write a poem about a Polish poet buried there. It was performed at the graveside, in a moving ceremony honouring the dead woman and her work.

Finally, a BBC radio producer who Tania had previously worked with suggested a radio documentary about the cemetery and singleness, interwoven with poems and conversation. The programme was broadcast on Radio 4 and the World Service, to critical acclaim.

What began as a creative whim ended in a new publication and valuable experience, raised her profile and generated income.

You don't have to do this alone. Use an existing relationship to grow a placement organically. If you love a particular museum, charity or shopping mall, approach them. They may have a budget for community engagement. Offer a proposal: suggest poems on postcards, Facebook reels or a live performance. The more work you do, the more frequently you will find those people and those places. Perhaps you have worked with a local school or festival: could they fund a short residency? If there is no money, then research grants and apply for them. If you get rejected, start again. After all, you are a poet. You should be used to rejection by now.

In the absence of funding, an unpaid residency is a low-risk way to build up your practice. I began by offering landscape poems to a Peak District tourism website. They were glad to have a poem every month; I got a new audience, and helpful deadlines for poems that I wanted to write anyway. Financial reward: none. Professional reward: moderate. Creative reward: very worthwhile. A self-built residency is a blisteringly good way of developing skills, contacts and experience which you can later use to attract paid work. Or do it just to serve your community. There is no mystical gatekeeper keeping you from these opportunities; make them happen.

There are two other sorts of residency. The first is advertised as a 'writing residency' which, when you look closely, turns out to be an 'opportunity' for you to pay for a stay in a lovely location. It may well nurture your writing, but you can do the same thing more cheaply by booking an Airbnb.

The second is one that pays you to actually reside somewhere, writing for your own ends. These are sanctuaries for the working unicorn. One is provided by the Hosking Houses Trust, for women over 40 who have published two books. Cove Park is a Scottish retreat which makes occasional grants for poets to live in isolated lakeside cabins and work on anything they like. The residency programme at Gladstone Library is again for published writers. Look up Hawthornden Castle, which essentially puts you in creative isolation with no wi-fi (oh, happy day!) and brings you dinner on a tray.

If you meet the criteria for these or others of the same kind, then I beg you to apply. Please don't tell yourself that you don't stand a chance. Some barriers are very real, but many more are obstacles that we place in our own path to spare ourselves disappointment. Don't second-guess the people who make the decision; kick your reservations out of the way, sit down and write an application.

On self-doubt, and unicorns

A professional residency makes you a conduit for others' emotions or aspirations. Be proud of your craft – and expect others to respect it too, because they usually do. I know, I know: you feel, at least some of the time, that you are kidding yourself. You feel that your family or day job erodes your creative life to the point of destruction; that others are better qualified to write, to think, to live the life of a poet.

These thoughts are not obstacles to being a poet: they are *preconditions*. Every one of those self-doubting, self-protecting, self-defeating strategies is another proof that you are the kind of vulnerable, questioning soul that ends up writing masterpieces. Bad luck. It comes with the territory.

Your powers of writing – those very powers that you question – sometimes look to other people like a mystical gift. Here's Dan Simpson, veteran of many residencies:

> It's like being a vessel. Being in this place, with these people, and then giving it back through my voice, my body, my thinking – but not colouring it too much with myself. It's very different to writing a poem for myself.

Reader, you are a creative unicorn. Consider yourself not lucky, but as entitled as any one else, to take up space as a professional creative. Go forth, and reside!

ACTIVITY: Build your own residency

- Identify a place or organisation you'd like to work with: a refugee charity, a stately home, a garden centre.
- Think about what you can offer, and what they might need. You could write poems for the shop wall, work with dementia patients to write about their experience or do a festival poetry trail.
- Work out your costs. Writing time, video editing time, planning time, travel time, time on site. Don't cheat yourself, make it viable. Add costs for printing posters. What's the total budget?
- Funding homework: research local or national grants that might cover your residency. Talk to your local writer development agency and Arts Council office. Consider crowdfunding.
- Now pick up the phone. Call your venue. Start talking to them.

Degna Stone

Unfolding, Meandering and Falling: The Art of Responding to a Commission

Introduction

I love wandering around museums and galleries to find inspiration for writing. Engaging with someone else's interpretation of the world often unlocks something in my subconscious that begins to form the seed of a poem. Writing 'in response to' creates the chance to explore preoccupations from a slant angle, providing a way in to writing that avoids the obvious (or most comfortable) route. It always feels like a gift when I'm invited to write a poem for a museum or gallery.

Writing to a brief is challenging but having parameters to work within can often free up the creative part of my mind, tapping into the subjects that I'm constantly drawn to in a way that feels out of reach when I'm left to my own devices. When writing in response to a commission from an art gallery or museum, I'll browse through any information that I've been given and maybe read through some ekphrastic poetry for inspiration (Auden's 'Musee des Beaux Arts' is perhaps one of the most famous). If I'm responding to a particular artwork or object, I'll research around the artist/maker but I'll also write in response to the way the artwork or object makes me feel. Those early emotional reactions often spark a train of thought that leads to a line of poetry to build on.

I consider everything that surrounds the object I'm responding to – the building, the location, current affairs – as I allow my mind to wander. Navigating museums with dozens of objects (or thousands in the case of Pitt Rivers Museum in Oxford) provides tons of inspiration and it's important to be open to all the musings that fleet through your mind – however trivial or seemingly unrelated. That's the approach that I took to three of the commissioned poems which ended up in my first collection and which I'll explore here.

'Vörður' responded to a residency at Gröndalshus in Reykjavik. 'Red Light' responded to Sean Scully's painting *Red Light*, exhibited as part of a retrospective of his work at The Laing and Hatton galleries in Newcastle upon Tyne. 'Proof of Life on Earth' responded to the collection at the Pitt Rivers Museum in Oxford.

Vörður

In 2017, I was invited to spend a week at Gröndalshus, a museum in Iceland. The brief was to create a multi-authored poem (alongside poets from Sweden, Iceland and the Faroe Islands) that would be accompanied by a film by the Icelandic artist María Dahlberg. We started the residency with a tour of the very windy harbour before heading to the museum – the former home of poet and naturalist Benedikt Gröndal. The house (which no longer stood in its original location) was built from a shipwrecked cargo of timber that had been salvaged at Hafnir on the Reykjanes peninsula in 1881. On the first afternoon of the residency, we decided to head out to Reykjanes to see where the timber landed and to find inspiration for the week ahead. The Icelandic landscape is elemental. Out on the peninsula the terrain feels timeless, almost extra-terrestrial. Once you move away from the road, the only signs of human activity were the vörður (cairns) dotted at intervals along the paths leading to the cliff edge. These details ended up in the commissioned poem in some form or other.

> The wind grows fierce at Reykjanes.
> We don't know where to begin so we wind
> our way across the ash-black landscape.

The direction this particular commission might take was completely open to us as poets. We could create whatever we wanted. Great! Except when all options are open to you, the freedom can feel debilitating. Alongside the weight of expectation from the commissioning organisation (whether real or perceived), the blank page can seem insurmountable. At an evening poetry reading at Grödhalshus, I confessed to a visual artist (Haraldur Jónsson) that I was convinced I wouldn't be able to produce anything useful during the residency. He'd also been creating collaborative work in a short space of time but he had only three days to our five. He described the process of creating like falling, you grab on to anything you can, if it works you keep hold of it, if it doesn't you let go. Eventually you'll get to the back to solid ground and you'll have created something. The trick is not to panic.

The conversations that I had in the various places I visited during the residency also informed my thinking about my poem. Some of elements of those conversations found their ways into the poems. Like a passing comment from an Icelandic poet about how an early morning dip in a freezing ocean can bring you back to your senses.

> We meet ourselves coming back from the edge
> of our senses. Feel the emptiness more than ever.

You never know what might provide inspiration, so capture as much as you can in your notebook and see what turns itself into poetry.

Red Light

In 2018, I was one of eight poets commissioned by Newcastle Poetry Festival to write poems in response to a Sean Scully retrospective at the Laing and Hatton galleries in Newcastle. The other poets included Imtiaz Dharker, the late Ciaran Carson and several other giants of contemporary poetry. No pressure then. We were given a pdf of the exhibition catalogue and invited to choose a painting: I selected *Red Light* and kept the festival theme of 'crossings' as an anchor point as I began to work on the poem. I thought about the crossing from living to dead. I thought about the borders between the haves and have-nots.

I live near Newcastle so I was able to visit *Red Light* as often as I needed. When I stood in front of the painting, I was struck by its size. The experience of being in the Laing Art Gallery is one that you don't often experience in larger cities: you can find yourself alone more often than not with nothing but the sound of the aircon unit to accompany your thoughts. The painting itself reminded me of a tower block viewed from a distance. We were coming up to the first anniversary of the Grenfell Tower disaster and the lack of accountability and justice alongside the devastating loss of life kept swirling around my mind as I looked at the painting.

> You shrink until the painting holds the menace
> of a tower block, with all the horror that brings
> The thought of being trapped, being afraid to die.
>
> To calm yourself, you count the colours, count the lines,
> try to figure out which was laid down first.
> You want to disappear into this painting.

I can't remember how many times I visited *Red Light*, three or four I think. Each time I would spend as long as possible with the painting, staring and thinking and imagining. After each visit, I would sit in my car in the side street next to the Laing and free-write, trying to capture everything that had cycled through my mind. I made notes about the composition, the techniques, the little things that I hadn't noticed at first. Like the fact that the background of the painting was not a block of colour; that it didn't follow the same geometry of the red lines that dominated the painting. There was a gentleness, a fluidity that created a tension.

> You wait until you are completely alone
> then cross the border of the painting,
> picking your way under each stripe of acrylic,
>
> challenging yourself to travel further in
> until you reach the ground, the first layer of paint,
> with its complexity of colour, its sinuous waves.

Not all my thoughts made it into the poem, in fact most didn't. From the pages and pages of freewriting, I transferred around 600 words into a Word document and the poem began to unfold itself as I selected lines. The start of the poem settled relatively early in the drafting process but the ending kept shifting. I'd been trying to wrap things up, trying to help the reader draw a conclusion, but once I stopped doing that the poem began to resolve itself.

The fulcrum of the poem is the line: "You want to disappear into this painting." A simple line that shifts the reader from static observer, paralysed by world events, to the protagonist of the poem. It sets them on a journey as the speaker walks with them as they try to come to terms with 'avoidable disasters', trying to find a way to live in a world that we can't escape from.

Proof of Life on Earth

In 2019, I was commissioned to write a piece based on the fascinating and problematic collection at Pitt Rivers Museum in Oxford. At the time I was reeling from the news that my mother-in-law's cancer was going to kill her. The unsettling feeling of being suddenly faced with the imminent death of a loved one consumed me as I travelled on the train from Newcastle to Oxford.

> In the museum of half a million objects
> my eyes don't know where to settle,
> so I lose myself amongst the maze of cases.

> Every surface is covered, every cabinet
> packed with artefacts, acquisition numbers
> tattooed conspicuously in precise white paint.
>
> The guide says much of the collection
> relates to how to attract a loved one,
> how to survive, how to deal with grief —

The meandering nature of exploring the museum was echoed in the poem, moving from one thought to the next, one object to the next. I added details that were true and details that weren't (the guide never said that the objects related to grief) in order to make the poem work for me. I incorporated the fact that I was forbidden from handling the objects I'd originally wanted to focus on (a medieval sword and a handgun). I used the alternatives that I'd been offered as a way to think about the feeling of being thrown into a pit of grief, even though the person I was grieving was still alive. Premature grief is a horrible thing that stops you living in the moment, stops you appreciating the life that is still being lived.

> There is a broadsword too heavy to carry,
> and a Walther PP, too dangerous to be placed
> in the hands of a poet. Objects out of bounds.
>
> Instead I study a single late medieval boot,
> one hundred hobnails hammered into its sole,
> and a brass aquamanile in the form of a horse.

When I left the museum for my return journey, the day was gloriously sunny but evidence of a world in tumult was all around. So many details that had been captured in my notebook didn't make their way into the poem because I couldn't find a way of doing them justice or because I felt that to use them would risk being exploitative or voyeuristic.

On the train journey home, the phrase 'proof of life on earth' suggested itself as a title for the poem. With that, something clicked into place and the final edits became much easier. The title brought an element to the poem that encapsulates the vast, unmanageable feelings I'd been experiencing during the writing process.

Conclusion

Writing poems in response to outside stimuli is useful for when you feel like the creative muse has gone on a bit of a hiatus (whether that's a commission or a prompt from a magazine or poetry competition). It's a great way of generating material as you always come up with far more phrases and images than you can use. In fact, I often discard at least 95% of the words I gather when writing my way into a poem. In the spirit of waste not want not, I take all the lines that don't make it into the final poem and put them into a 'soup'. I can't remember where I first came across the idea of a 'soup' page but it must have been in a workshop somewhere along the line. My 'soup' is usually a double-page spread at the back of my notebook (I also have a digital version). Soup pages create eyeball kicks, juxtapositions that might lead to something completely unexpected. Soup pages give you the permission to strip favourite lines out of a poem if they no longer fit the poem without fear of losing them forever. The fragments of lines and images wait patiently until the next time I am in need of some inspiration. I'll have a read through and see if there are any lines that might spark something new.

I'm often surprised by the poems that have been written in response to a commission. They don't always work as standalone pieces but, when they do, they tap into something unexpected and present themselves to you like a gift.

Addendum

It's lovely to be commissioned to write a poem or invited to be 'in residence' but when you're starting out these opportunities rarely fall in your lap. Depending on where you're at with your writing you might want to reach out to museums and galleries and ask them if they have any openings for a poet/writer in residence. If you're earlier on in your career, make sure you're signed up to the mailing list of your closest writing development organisation (e.g. New Writing North, Writing West Midlands, etc.) as they'll often list opportunities for new writers.

ACTIVITY

1. Visit an exhibition (in-person or online).
2. Choose an object or work.
3. Spend as long as your circumstances allow just looking at it.
4. Let your mind wander. Think about the things that enrage you or fill you with joy (or tap into another intense emotion).
5. Find somewhere away from the work and spend ten minutes writing down everything that comes to mind. Don't pause, don't edit.
6. When ten minutes is up, highlight any phrases or images that surprise or delight you. This is your first draft.
7. Leave the draft alone for at least a week.
8. After a week has passed, revisit your draft. Maybe you'll be lucky and it's already a poem. More likely, this will be the first of many drafts.
9. Let yourself be surprised as the poem begins to emerge.
10. Enjoy the process.

Daisy Henwood & Lewis Buxton

How to Make Toast:
Producing Poetry Events

TOAST is a monthly poetry night in Norwich. Our primary goal is to entertain audiences with poetry. We want to make something worth returning to, something that lasts, something that brings people together and provides a platform for some of the best poetry in the world. This checklist is how we make it worthwhile for people to come out on a Sunday night in winter to listen to poetry they could probably read at home.

Venue
Find a room. For free if you can. This is your first step: without a venue, there is no event. We have worked in lots of different venues over the years, from professional art centres to toilet-smelling pub basements. It's all about how you work with the space you've got.

Work out the capacity of your venue early on and stick to it: if it's 20 people max, don't cram in another 10. Equally, if you've landed yourself a 1500 seat venue, how will you fill the space? Other questions to ask yourself about the venue:

- Is it accessible?
- Is it comfortable?
- How will the seats be arranged? Can everyone see?
- Is there a sound bleed? Can you hear Darren and Michelle's anniversary party kicking off through the pub's thin wall?

Poetry can be uncomfortable enough; people should be physically comfortable whilst it's happening. Of course, we are so often constrained by the limits of what is free or affordable, but this does not have to mean the space cannot be made comfortable.

Artists

Booking poets is a highlight of the job. You get to decide, out of all the poets that exist in the world, who you would like headlining your event.

Our first piece of advice is, allow yourself to ask anyone. Anyone. The worst the poet laureate can say is no (and he did).

Secondly, and we'll say this over and over again, think about your audience: what experience do you want them to have? Do you want Joelle Taylor, who'll give you a poetry set that is more like an anthem? Do you want Rob Auton's quiet hilarity? Do you want a set that is half pub chat, half call to arms, à la Yomi Ṣode? Or do you want Theresa Lola to gently explain who Ja Rule is to 100 people in Norfolk? (All have happened at TOAST, all were amazing).

If you have more than one poet on the bill, how do they fit together? Is it too jarring an experience to have a laugh-out-loud set of poetry and rapping, followed by a sombre reflection on the climate crisis? Maybe this is exactly what you want – but make sure you know the work of the poets you are booking, and have some sense of their style and what they bring to the stage. Think also about the range of performers you're booking: it is important for an audience to see themselves reflected on stage. In order to attract a broad audience, you need a diverse and inclusive range of poets.

Audience Experience

Think about your audience. Again. Give them a reason to come to your poetry show.

Everything from the poets you book to the way you set up the stage to how comfortable the chairs are plays into how an audience will feel walking into the space. And, as much as possible, there should *always* be a bar. (See the exercise at the end of this essay for ways to think about your poetry show's vibe).

We often also give a general trigger warning – just to let our audience know that the poets might bring up difficult topics, and that no one in the room will judge someone for needing to step out. Above all, we want our audience to feel safe, welcome, and seen. Remember, poetry events aren't just for poets – that is what workshops, writing groups and symposiums on whether or not we are working in a 'dead' artform are for. Think about your audience, and when you're done, think about them some more.

Marketing

For us, this is the worst bit of the job. If you have any room in your budget, hire someone else to do this for you. Sometimes, though, you can't do that, so here are a couple of tips for marketing without the meltdowns:

Communicate the basics: who, what, where, and when.

- Give a sense (via branding, photos, captions, where you choose to leave your leaflets/posters) of what your event will be like. If you're going for a slick, sophisticated vibe, a poster in Comic Sans isn't going to communicate that.
- Utilise social media. But also think outside the digital box. We put up posters in charity shops, leave leaflets in cafes, and go to other poetry and arts events in the city to talk to people about what we do.
- Invest in local communities. Go out and find your audience, and find organisations that can help with this. Who are the community leaders? How can you extend your reach?
- Our number one goal with TOAST is to bring people to poetry events who wouldn't usually come. Converting a poetry sceptic is one of the biggest joys of the job, and it's only possible if we go to where the poets aren't.

Operations

Operations is everything from budgets to box office to bar staff. How much is your event going to cost? What are you going to pay the poets (if at all)? What are the poets' travel arrangements? Where do the audience check in? What time does the event start? How do people get into the venue? And where is the funding coming from? Ticket sales? Arts Council England? Local sponsorship? Like editing in films, the intricacies of poetic form, or the work of NHS staff in the UK, this is the stuff that no one notices, but without it, everything falls apart.

Tech & Set

The great thing about putting on a poetry night, as opposed to, say, a music gig, is that the technical requirements are very low. You just need to make sure your performers can be seen and heard. Depending on your venue, all of the tech might be provided, which makes your job much easier. Regardless, here are some things to think about:

- Have a microphone and a PA. And always do a sound check. This will avoid a "can you hear me at the back?" moment at the start of your show.
- Play music – background or entrance music – through good speakers. It puts the audience at ease.
- Teach new performers how to use a microphone! There's nothing more frustrating than watching a good performance that you can't hear.
- Use stage lights, lamps, or fairy lights to draw focus to your stage. Similarly, have some kind of set – a banner, a backdrop, a table with props. The audience will know where to look, and the poets won't feel lost.

Opt, as much as possible, for simplicity. It's better to do one or two things well than bodge a complicated set up. We are not technicians. We can set up our simple PA, run the music, and sort out our lights, but it's enough.

Hosting

A host brings the audience into the show. They introduce the poets, warm up the crowd, and ensure everything runs smoothly.

It's the host's job to take the hit of a few last people walking in, someone at the bar ordering too loudly, or the awkwardness of an audience who aren't used to poetry. We always think about Aimee Nezhukumatathil's poem 'Invitation,' which starts, "Come in, come in. The water's fine! You can't get lost / here." Welcoming people to a poetry event is not unlike convincing them to go cold water swimming – they're aware of how uncomfortable it might be, but once you break the initial coldness they have a brilliant time.

How are you, as a host, going to welcome people? Are you going to read them a poem? If so, what poem are you going to choose? Starting with a 'manifesto of masculinity and the mental health crisis' may not set the right tone – save it for the second half. Instead, do a poem about a dog, the local park, loud people in the quiet carriage. Make people laugh, maybe think a little, get them used to being spoken to. Sometimes you have to teach them how to listen and respond. To be a host is to be a sacrificial lamb, a swimming teacher and, sometimes, Bridget Jones, when she introduces people at publishing parties with two interesting facts about each of them. It's okay to be the fool for a minute or two; take the audience, the event, the other poets seriously, but perhaps not yourself.

The Show

There are as many ways of running a show as there are of writing a poem: is it an open mic to hold the beautiful voices of your local community of poets? Is it an exclusive, invite-only cabaret club of poets smoking cigarettes like they are in a 19th century French salon? Or, in the case of TOAST, it is a tight 2-hour show (more than enough time for poetry magic to happen, and it stops the audience getting fidgety) with two headliners performing 25 minute sets and three pre-booked new poets doing 5 minutes each? Remember, live performance will always be different on stage than it is on a timesheet: if you've given open mic-ers 5 minutes (and be very clear that means 5 *minutes*) then you have to remember the time it takes to get on and off stage, for the audience's rapturous applause, for you to wipe away a tear at a particularly emotional poem. Build in time for yourself: no one wants to still be in the venue at 1am because six poets haven't managed to get on stage yet. Ultimately, if you've done all of the prep, the show should run itself. Your artists have arrived, your stage is set up, your audience have already bought the tickets and you know exactly how everything will run.

Watch the audience – see what they enjoy, and what they don't. And try as much as possible to enjoy the poetry.

Packing Down
It's hard to follow this advice (we only follow it half of the time) but try to put away your gear in a way that will make unpacking it for the next show as easy as possible. Wind up cables, store your set, get rid of anything you don't need. Then you can go to the pub safe in the knowledge that you've done your future self a massive favour. And think about how you're getting everything back to where it needs to be. We've done everything from carry home three huge bags full of cardboard set and electrical equipment from the pub at 1am, to very sensibly parking around the corner from the show and abstaining from post-show beers. Whatever you do, having a plan in mind makes it easier to have fun and unwind after the show.

Next Steps
Pause for a second and reflect on what you just made happen. When the show is over, you may find yourself heading to the pub or somewhere equally fun (like home to bed). Congratulate yourself on a job well done.

We try for an informal debrief the next day, to take stock of what we really enjoyed, and what could be improved for next time. This is also a good time to gauge general audience reactions. It is always good to hear from audience members, or see what they've posted on Instagram, because it's all about them and their experience, after all.

When you're done with the show, let yourself be done. Have a look over the photos, think about what you liked, and give yourself a little break. Putting on regular events can feel like a hamster wheel – allow the good feelings from the previous show to propel you towards the next one, but give yourself some down time before you head back to step 1 and do it all again.

Conclusion

In the same way we don't all have to write sonnets, or do long-form one person shows, we don't all have to produce poetry shows. But if you do, those shows are all as different and multifaceted as poetry itself. There is no one clear way to do it (though we would argue there are several ways *not* to do it: don't let it go on too long; don't exclude people from the event; don't keep the entire door money for yourself in a complicated embezzling scheme).

The best advice we can give you is to care about your event. Care about your poets, your venue, your audience, and yourself. Don't run yourself into the ground and stress out over how many people show up. We've travelled hundreds of miles, spent lots of money, and had many arguments in the car on the way to rural shows where only four people came. But guess what? They were really good shows. Yes, things fall apart: the mic stand does not hold. Something will break, trains will be late, and your headliner will get ill. You'll forget that one cable and your host will trip over on stage and knock the set over. But it will be fine. There is no such thing as an emergency in poetry, and poetry audiences are kind. The thing that will make you feel better about all of this is who you choose to work with. Pick someone who makes you laugh, who supports you, and who likes the parts of the job that you don't.

Rebecca Solnit says that "making a poem is like making a chair: a poem is as real as a chair, and sometimes more useful." The same goes for poetry events. They are made things; they are useful to us in this world. We make them every month. It's not always as simple as making toast, but oftentimes, it's as warm, as comforting, and as important.

So good luck. Have a good time. Make something happen.

ACTIVITY: Perfect Poetry Night

Imagine your ideal poetry night – as an audience member, performer, or producer. Go for real pie-in-the-sky scenarios: where is it happening? Who is headlining? How long is it, how many people are there, and what refreshments are available?

This kind of thinking is a fun way of getting to what you really value in a poetry night – if your ideal event is in a submarine with twenty other people, then maybe you want to book the old wine cellars and deck them out with fairy lights. Equally, if your ideal event happens at the Apollo with big sparkly lights, then you want somewhere with flair and built-in tech opportunities.

No ideas are too big or too silly: write them all down in a long list, then go back through the list and think about how each item would translate into an actually achievable poetry event.

Works Cited:
Aimee Nezhukumatathil, 'Invitation,' *Oceanic* (Copper Canyon Press, 2018), p. 29.

Rebecca Solnit, *The Faraway Nearby* (Granta, 2013), p. 72.

Jaqueline Saphra

The Theatre of Poetry
and the Poetry of Theatre

I love a good story. I know that when I haven't got a novel on the go, one that I can't wait to return to for what happens next, my life feels half empty. I know the importance of stories in giving shape to universal experiences, how civilisations through the ages have relied on them to make sense of a random universe. I'm thinking of poetic narratives like ballad, an early form that was easy to remember through its metre and rhyme, and held its audience through storytelling; I'm thinking of dramatic monologues like Browning's riveting 'My Last Duchess' that relies heavily on narrative, voice and diction. I am of course aware that poetry is not expected to pay homage to narrative; in fact, very often contemporary poets are discouraged from the shaped and linear structure of a good tale well told.

These are vast generalisations and you could always find examples to the contrary. But between lyric and experimental modes in contemporary poetry, the modern world is frequently embodied through fragmentation, dissociation, juxtaposition. Where a Shakespearean tragedy, or a Shakespearean sonnet makes strenuous efforts to firmly tie up the ending to leave us satisfied, the contemporary poem or play will tend to leave an audience dangling on the end of an untied ribbon, or, to use another metaphor, to leave the door open and refuse a sense of closure.

I recently saw Simon Stone's reimagining of *Phaedra*, a classic Greek drama from two thousand years ago, at the National Theatre in which the play was given a modern setting. The playwright seemed to be working inordinately hard to stay true to the Aristoleian definition of tragedy. He attempted to force the play towards the original ending by bringing it to its cathartic and shattering climax: in the original story, Phaedra falls in love with her stepson Hippolytus and, when rejected, she lies that he raped her. Her husband then asks the god Poseidon to kill Hippolytus, and Phaedra kills herself. In a contemporary setting, this final act looked faintly ridiculous and almost impossible to believe despite the actress's valiant efforts to make it credible. It made me think about the difficulties embodied in the Shakespearean sonnet with its neat, wrapped up final couplet. We are not living in an age of solutions, conclusions or tragic endings. I haven't done a study, but I'd wager that contemporary poets, when they do embrace the classic sonnet form, will tend to go for the Petrarchan sonnet with its eight line/six line imbalance and the less obvious final couplet. This is more appropriate, perhaps, to the times.

***

I knew for most of my life that I wanted to be a writer. By my late teens, I had tried my hand at short fiction, novels (two really bad ones), songwriting, poetry and plays. Finally, I fell in love with theatre and read Drama at university; and somewhere in a drawer, I even have a certificate to prove I completed a postgraduate diploma in playwriting.

After university, I carried on working in my own way, mainly relying on the practical work I had done with my peer group where I had been writing and directing my own plays. The degree had been valuable in many ways, but the main lessons were in the art of collaboration and learning through low-stakes failures and successes on the job.

In those days, there was very little structured support for training new writers, but, after I moved home to London, I was instantly picked up by a major literary agent and commissioned by several theatre companies. I had no idea how lucky I was.

Not that it was easy, or that I took the work for granted – it was a baptism of fire and I once went to bed for a week after one coruscating review in a major newspaper.

Eventually life intervened and I spent a few years mostly consumed by motherhood. Although I tried to keep the writing going, it was a very stop-start affair and I lost momentum and footing. This is a common experience for women and explains why so many women writers get a late start in their professional life.

At some point in the 1990s, I applied for a short, funded course in screenwriting at The National Film School, thinking this might give me a kick-start back into writing. It gave me a bigger kick than I expected, because I went on to be one of the few participants offered a place on their inaugural screenwriting course, which proved to be a true baptism of fire – we were a competition-fuelled, driven and fractious group and the teaching was fairly brutal. I survived this, however, even though I was pregnant again, and went on to take many meetings with various film companies. These led to unfulfilled promises and madness-years in development hell and a decision to give it all up, followed by a distressingly long and fallow period. It had taken me nearly a decade to understand that wasn't suited to screenwriting, where the words are probably the least important part, where the script is a blueprint for the final cut, where the story is what matters most. You would have thought I'd love that, obsessed as I am with narrative. But no. Because I love language just as much.

I hated not writing. I hated the emptiness of my life without the obsessive lure of pen and paper.

But just when I thought it was all over, something happened. I distinctly remember the day I was rescued by poetry. A poem – not a very good one – suddenly arrived fully formed. It was called 'What Can I Write in Fifteen Minutes?' because that was all

I had. I've been sharing my life with poetry ever since, although I'm still devoted to my other crush: theatre.

It wasn't until 2016 that I found myself wondering if I could combine my two great loves. I had found ways to collaborate with artists and composers and other poets. I missed that most collaborative of artforms, theatre which, after all has its roots in poetry going back as far the Ancient Greeks. Shakespeare himself was a poet and not ashamed to show that he was. I remember being amazed to discover that there are whole sonnets embedded in *Romeo and Juliet*:

> [Romeo] If I profane with my unworthiest hand
> This holy shrine, the gentle fine is this:
> My lips, two blushing pilgrims, ready stand
> To smooth that rough touch with a tender kiss.

> [Juliet] Good pilgrim, you do wrong your hand too much,
> Which mannerly devotion shows in this;
> For saints have hands that pilgrims' hands do touch,
> And palm to palm is holy palmers' kiss.

> [Romeo] Have not saints lips, and holy palmers too?

> [Juliet] Ay, pilgrim, lips that they must use in prayer.

> [Romeo] O, then, dear saint, let lips do what hands do;
> They pray, grant thou, lest faith turn to despair.

> [Juliet] Saints do not move, though grant for prayers' sake.

> [Romeo] Then move not, while my prayer's effect I take.

> (*Romeo and Juliet* Act I, Scene 5)

Just as our theatrical ancestors didn't distinguish between dialogue and poetry, some of our finest modern dramatists –

Sarah Kane, Alice Birch and Annie Baker, for example – write in highly poetic modes. In 2014, Mike Bartlett wrote a play in blank verse: *Charles III* is about a constitutional crisis on the accession of Charles to the throne. Carol Ann Duffy's *Everyman* for the National Theatre included different poetic idioms including rap, blank verse and heroic couplets.

I was re-inspired, thinking about poetic modes and voices, wondering how to harness my hard-won craft skills. A monologue, the form of most lyric poems, seemed a useful start and I began to write *The Noises*, a play in the voice of a dog. The speaker was modelled on my own rescue dog, Lola (Luna in the play), and, drawing on what little we knew of her experience, I thoroughly and enthusiastically anthropomorphised her. The dog voice enabled me to write a play grounded in primal feelings and impulses: love, hunger, terror, rage. I was able to embed one large story and several small ones inside the play, which allowed me to indulge my love of narrative. And all the time I was playing with language, trying to work out the diction and thought progressions of a being who was a human-animal hybrid. This gave me huge and heavenly latitude.

I was fortunate to have my own homegrown dramaturg and director (my daughter Tamar Saphra) to bring the play to life after a successful Arts Council application, and I was especially proud that the production was accessible to people who were blind or visually impaired. It is worth mentioning here that you don't need to wait for a theatre to stage your play for you; you can do it yourself, especially if it's a monologue (fewer moving parts, lower costs).

This is an excerpt from the beginning of the play where Luna the dog has been locked in a dark room because she has eaten the family's lunch. You'll notice that I scored it for the music and made use of the white space as if it were a poem:

The chicken, the chicken! I find it waiting. Must be for me I say it's on the table near my mouth and nobody else there to eat it and so I get a leg mmmm mmmm. And I crunch and I grrrr and I swallow and it's my day my day of chew and crunch.

And I wait

and I look

and the chicken got only one leg so I get the other one to make it pretty and then what's the use of a chicken with no legs?

Maybe it was the sick; chickens all juice and easy swallow but they got little sharp crack crack in the mouth and I'm in a speed in case they catch me

so I gobble and push it down, push it down.

I learn that since a pup. Never share!

But then there's the sharp gets stuck in the neck of me and I'm ggggg ggggg cckkkkk and then out comes the sharp and all the chicken is soup and it smells so good while it's falling out of me.

So the soupy chicken's all on the carpet and it's sweet on my nose and I roll in it, roll in it! Mmmm.

Ma won't like that and she'll take it away and cover the carpet with the burny stuff so I fix it! Quick quick quick and I lap up the sicky soupy chicken and it smells so mmmmmmmm and I'm lapping lapping oh happy me, happy happy me.

Look what I did.

I fix it!

I fix it all by myself.

I'm good!

And as I worked my way through Luna's story, I found myself thinking more deeply about narrative and character and voice about the differences between poetry and theatre

white space
ambiguity
openness
the explosive ruinous creative subjectivity of art
Why we do it
who we do it for

***

I teach poetry and many of our discussions revolve around

> what the poem is
>> what the poet 'means'(which they often don't know,
> which is fine)
> how the poem is received

Part of my job is to open up the possibility that once a poem is out there on the page a poet can let it go
>> it belongs then to the reader
> & the reader's perception is the reader's perception
how brilliant, I always say – as one reader disagrees with another
about a poem – to have different views in the room
some love the poem, some hate it, some are indifferent
> some connect with it, some don't
some want it to be more direct, some want it to be more opaque
some are happy with multiple levels of interpretation & ambiguity & some find that harder to tolerate.
& what a boring world it would be if we all agreed

***

For *The Noises*, the most contentious debates came from the deliberate choices we as a team made to allow space and ambiguity:

> Audiences variously
>> embraced the ambiguity
>>> enjoyed filling in the spaces themselves
>>>> been delighted to be left with questions
>>>>> found the openness confusing
> or distracting
> Some like to have meanings & events pinned down & fully explained
>> Some don't

Some have been so caught up with the character, voice & fate of
Luna and for some, none of those concerns have been relevant
Some have concentrated on the ethical & political questions the
play poses – the animal in all of us & how that manifests.

**

As a playwright friend wrote to me after seeing *The Noises:* "You
poets are never knowingly 'on the nose'." '

**

Poets might feel as if the poem is out of their control once it's on
the page – but ha ha ha …
    the playwright will scoff at the poet's fears
        because the poet has the luxury of delivering
their work fully formed to an audience
    but the play is live & temporary & therefore unstable
the play is performed in space & time & then it's gone
        the poem exists until the page itself disintegrates
& even then it may exist fully in the mind of its reader

**

    the poem has a uniquely private relationship with its reader
        the play is a collective experience

**

the play is a concrete *thing* composed of people & objects & three
dimensions – not only words
    the poem is a 'machine made of words' & words only

**

the play is a collaborative creation, born of many mothers
        of whom the playwright is only one
    the play does not exist until it is fully realised on the stage
        You may spend years (as I did) growing the

script, but the making-rollercoaster really happens in the last breathless downhill twenty seconds of its life when the script is birthed by its multiple mothers as your rickety little car bumps & jolts down the hill

gaining momentum by the minute

you can never have total control because danger is the essence of the journey

***

I set out on a fundamentally insane mission: to write a play that's a hybrid poetry/theatre piece from the point of view of a talking dog

It existed for a brief period of time and then like a dream it was gone

the result of this mission carried in its bones all the joys, challenges & complications of both artforms

& I knew I was chancing it but what is art if not a giant risk?

ACTIVITY: Short prompt towards a first draft

Think of an animal with whom you have had an encounter or a relationship, whether this has been a positive experience or not. It may be, for example, your childhood guinea pig, a pet rabbit, an animal at the zoo, or a cat who may be sitting on your lap at this very moment.

Now explore the emotional life of this creature, get in touch with how they might feel. You may know something about the history of this animal, or you may just want to use your imagination – or both.

Think about the life they have led, the story or stories they might recount, stories that might echo or mirror more human experiences. What can they tell us about this world?

Consider their diction, the language that they might use and how it might differ from your own. How might they describe, for example, the stars or the bed, or flowers, or snow?

When you are ready, begin to write your play from the point of view of the animal you have chosen. It may take a few attempts for you to find the true voice. Experiment! Let the poem and the animal lead the way.

Roshni Beeharry

Taking Poetry into Unexpected Places: Writing with Healthcare Staff, Students, and Those with Health Conditions

Writing has been the main way I express myself for enjoyment since I was a child and, in time, I discovered its powerful potential for reflection and healing when I experienced my first loss of a family member. I did not write my first poem or read poetry (apart from at school) until the age of 26, a year after the death of my younger brother. Grief took charge, and like a well-meaning but firm friend, signalled to me that I really did have to stop and allow myself to process the overwhelming impact of losing my only sibling. It was during that dark time that I was introduced to the illuminating potential of poetry therapy – "the use of language, symbol, and story in therapeutic, educational, growth, and community-building capacities. It relies upon the poems, stories, song lyrics, imagery and metaphor to facilitate personal growth, healing, and greater self-awareness."

In this essay, I outline my journey into working with others using poetry and other forms of creative writing for self-expression, enjoyment, wellbeing and personal development, and offer some guidance and reflective learning points that I have gleaned experientially along the way.

Epiphany

Poetry can be a way of distilling emotions, experiences, reflections and musings, past and present. It is also a way of envisioning the future, exploring, experimenting, trying something out. For me, there is something freeing about not knowing quite where the words will take me, and without the pressure to 'make sense' in the form of prose.

Returning to writing at this very challenging time in my life, was a gift to myself. I found that by giving myself space and time to express my creativity once more, I was accessing the familiarity and the essence of who I am, which was instrumental at a time when I felt like I had lost myself.

I realised then that I could help those I cared for as a doctor, not just with my clinical skills, but by supporting others to discover the potentially healing aspects of creative writing for themselves. This discovery felt like an epiphany for me.

I went on to train formally in Writing for Wellbeing, also known as therapeutic writing or 'words for wellbeing'. This practice uses creative writing, poetry therapy, journalling, memoir, reflective writing and expressive writing (the writing of factual rather than creative material about a situation, pioneered by Professor James Pennebaker), to express emotions, experiences and reflections.

Unlike 'conventional' creative writing groups and workshops, the emphasis on this type of writing is on process – the emotions generated and experience of doing the writing, and reflection of the writing process as well as on what was written, more so than the product, be it a poem, story, or piece of memoir.

Working with others through poetry and writing
Over the last three decades, I have continued to immerse myself in the world of literature and hone my own writing in writing groups as a participant, and I now design and run writing for wellbeing and personal development workshops through my own organisation, Storied Selves (www.storiedselves.com). This work includes writing with those receiving care, e.g. those with mental health issues and with chronic pain. It also includes writing with those giving care to others, both professional and unpaid carers, both in groups and 1:1 including in my role as a creative writing tutor for a London-based charity that provides groups for unpaid carers over 50 years of age, drawing on my experience as an unpaid carer myself.

As a university medical educator, I have incorporated therapeutic and creative writing into research projects and modules created for medical students, and creative writing for their personal and professional development; I also provide workshops for NHS staff and social care staff, as well as community events, open to anyone, online and in person.

Considerations when setting up writing projects/groups within healthcare, including groups such as patients and service users: As a general principle, think about who you want to work with and what you can offer: there are ethical considerations when working with anyone of any age, but working with adults or children who have been defined as vulnerable, of course requires especially careful planning, including ethical considerations, including maintaining their wellbeing and safety. It is important to liaise closely with the manager/organiser/commissioner of the group you are setting up, and ensure you have the appropriate level of skills and qualifications to work with the particular group. If you are new to this area of work or to healthcare environments, it is essential you have a link member of staff who you can liaise with regularly before, during, and after the workshop or event, including visiting the place where your workshops will be carried out. Think carefully about your own motivation for doing this work. What do you want to offer and what do you want to gain from doing this work?

Set yourself a generous time frame to plan workshops – always allow extra time for unforeseen events and delays! Consider how much time you have alongside your job/family or other caring commitments/other commitments. Think carefully about the environment you will be working in. How will you be delivering the workshop? Will this be in person, online or in hybrid form, with some participants in the room with you and others online? Or even more challenging, some participants in a room with a co-facilitator and you hosting online? If you are facilitating the workshop in person, it is essential to visit the venue and meet the staff you will be working with if possible. Hospital and community health-centre environments can be hard to navigate if one is not familiar with them, so it's worth investing some time on this.

If hosting online, be confident that you have the technical skills and resources, including a reliable wi-fi connection for Zoom or chosen platform – and practice, practice, practice beforehand, even if you have the experience of working online! I spent over two years of the pandemic teaching medical students online as well as running writing for wellbeing groups online, and there was rarely a session that went without some sort of internet hitch! Being able to troubleshoot calmly is essential. This is where having a co-facilitator or online co-host who may not be involved in the group itself can be very helpful, particularly for large, online groups.

Finance
Consider the materials you will need, the cost implications and what you expect the participants to provide for themselves (i.e. notebooks and pens) and what the host/ organiser or venue, e.g. a hospital or care home, provide for you.

Will you charge for the workshops and, if so, how much? Will there be concessions? Or, is there funding from a commissioning body such as an NHS Trust, university, etc. Always ask, no one can be expected to work for free!

I recommend obtaining professional indemnity to protect yourself and participants legally for this type of work. In the UK, a Disclosure and Barring Service (DBS) check is essential when working with the public and adults who may be vulnerable, young people and children.

The group
Who are the participants? Young people, adults, those with health conditions, staff, students? Each will need specific considerations and planning, and careful selection of writing prompts and

material. Is it a closed group or open, drop-in group? How does this impact on the group dynamic and comfort of the participants not only to write, but to share personal work?

Establishing a group agreement and safeguarding wellbeing of participants is essential. A key role of a facilitator is to foster a safe and confidential space for any group setting, and when working with adults or children who have been defined as particularly vulnerable in some way. It is important to spend some time at the start of the group, after introductions are complete, to outline a consensus group agreement, which can be written for reference, including respectful listening and sharing, valuing all participant contributions and having the right to choose not to share or contribute at times, confidentiality and anonymity when discussing people from life, e.g. family, partners, peers or, in the case of those in the caring professions and students, patients or service users.

I like to use my own lived experience to inform the writing prompts I design, including an awareness that poetry is not for everyone. I therefore use a mixture of poetry and prose in my workshops. Many of us (including myself) have memories of having to interpret and learn poetry at school, and this may feel intimidating to some in adulthood, and even more so for those reading or writing a poem for the first time. It is important to give participants options, including permission to write what comes, or indeed write nothing at all.

When setting expectations for the group, acknowledge openly that writing and sharing can be challenging, especially for the first time. I have found it helpful to 'role model' some challenges that I personally had when joining a writing group, e.g. the trepidation of sharing writing and fearing of being judged, or feeling your writing is 'not good enough' – we have all experienced this at some point! This can help normalise that feeling, and make participants feel more at ease. Other ways to set expectations and dispel any misconceptions is to reassure participants that writing does not need to be polished or be finished. Many think that poems should rhyme – reassure them that *"whatever you write is right for you"*, a lovely mantra I have adopted from therapeutic writing peers. You may wish to share examples of your own poetry as well as published established poets as prompts.

Will you be critiquing writing in the group? If so, ensure this is clear in the first session (or start of the session, if you are only having one workshop with the group). Go through how to give feedback sensitively to each other with the participants. Although process rather than product is likely to be the emphasis in this type of writing, many participants come to writing groups expecting some feedback on their writing and/or technique. Think about how in depth you will be with your feedback and whether this is in your skill set. There are many ways to give feedback in writing groups – find a way that you have used yourself as a writing group participant or in your own training or learning. As the facilitator, it is your responsibility to moderate the sharing of work and participants giving feedback sensitively.

How frequent will the workshop be? Is it a one-off or a series? Knowing who your participants are will influence the design, resources, and timings in your workshop.

What are your expected outcomes? Will there be a performance? Maybe an anthology will be produced – if so, who will collate and print this? Again, consider cost implications.

Evaluation
Will you be evaluating the sessions? Think about the methods you will use and who you will be sharing the results with, as this may influence the choice of evaluation method. Given the population you are working with, you will need to ensure extracts of writing or any information shared is done so with

participants' consent, and anonymised to protect participants' confidentiality.

Practice what you preach and teach: ensuring your own wellbeing.
It can be a challenge to maintain your own writing practice when designing and facilitating groups for others, given the demands of life and other work.

As with any work supporting other people, ensure you look after yourself – maybe make time to debrief after in a reflective practice journal which can include prose, poetry and freewriting, doodles, anything which helps you process and develop.

Consider working with a mentor or supervisor experienced in this area or attend a peer supervision group or combine both approaches as I do. Lapidus International and many arts and health organisations are setting up support for arts practitioners in this area.

Case studies:
1. Writing with those receiving care in NHS settings and in the community.

Writing with those with chronic pain: MA Creative Writing & Personal Development dissertation project – an action research project entitled Creative Writing as an adjunct to Self-Management of Chronic Pain.

Participants: three patients admitted on an inpatient Chronic Pain Management Programme (PMP).

Workshops: weekly 1.5-hour workshops over three weeks.

Where: rehabilitation ward in a specialist tertiary hospital in London. The group took place in a room on the ward after patient dinner was finished, so at the end of the PMP day.

Poetry prompt used in this project: Charles Bukowski's poem, 'About Pain' (1983, in copyright) in Workshop 1, with the aim of encouraging the three participants to discuss their pain. Here's an extract from the poem:

> it's all so painful
> For me, each stroke
> Is pain ...
> one mistake and

I used this poem as a form of poetry therapy practice, that is, as a stimulus for the group to respond in writing, and then facilitated group discussion. I read it out loud and then asked the group to read it to themselves, and respond to it in writing. I then invited them to share their reflections and/or writing if they wished, as a facilitated group discussion. You can also ask participants to select a line and write a response or carry on writing from the end of the poem or another line, ensuring you give an option to write memoir, fiction, as well as poetry.

Reflections: This workshop was an example of 'knowing your audience', which isn't always possible before a workshop, but is important to anticipate the needs of the group, particularly when working with those with health conditions. It also helps guide you in selecting which writing exercises to use or to avoid. I had the advantage of being a trainee doctor on the Rehabilitation Unit ward for a year prior to the project, so I was able to anticipate some of the challenges and emotions that the participants would face from my clinical experience. E.g., fear of the loss of their normal lives and level of activities and fear they would never be the same with a sense of grief. This insight was instrumental in designing suitable writing exercises for each session. I also was aware that those with chronic pain cannot always sit for prolonged periods of time or write easily for prolonged periods, and hence I asked all participants before meeting them what the longest time they would be comfortable sitting for was, and used this to plan appropriate breaks for stretches and refreshment, etc.

If you are running a workshop in healthcare that is not related to a research project, then you do not need to go through the formal Research and Ethics process as I had to, but it is essential to check with the person who has asked or commissioned you to run the workshop, who may be a manager, senior member of staff, hospital arts department or volunteers department, as there will be other protocol to follow, to ensure patient/service user safety in this environment.

2. Writing with those giving care to others: creative writing for wellbeing and personal development workshop, and a GP training programme hub day.

Theme: community, isolation and connection.

Audience: 46 GP trainees (qualified doctors undertaking a three-year specialist programme to become GPs) and five GP training programme leads (practicing senior GPs with training responsibility as well as clinical experts).

Venue: online via Zoom.

Rationale for theme: COVID-19 left many of us feeling isolated. Healthcare staff at the frontline were particularly isolated from their families and from their colleagues, with a move to working online and telephone as GPs, and in particular training grade GPs who were often the only trainee in a practice in a large geographical area, lacking the usual face-to-face peer support by contemporaries. This theme was discussed with the lead GP who was responsible for training. It is important to hone the design of the workshop on what the participant or their representative specify, in this case the GP trainees and GP training programme lead, so it is imperative to invest time in communicating with them, and I find it helpful to send a draft workshop plan.

Poetry prompt used: I found that a gentle way to introduce writing, particularly as the majority of the GPs were new to creative writing, was to ask the group to attempt to freewrite, also known as stream of consciousness writing. This can take the form of writing to a theme or whatever comes into their head, or to a suggested word or image, for a timed period. The writing does not need to be shared, and participants should always be made aware of this before writing, with the aim of removing self-censorship as much as possible so the participants know they can write what they wish and no one else will see it or hear it.

In this group, I suggested the phrase 'connection means…' to use if they wished, setting a timer for five minutes. They were then invited to read over what they had written, underlining words that resonated, repeated, surprised them or perturbed them. They were each asked to share just two words or phrases in that process with the group and a collaborative list was created. Finally, the group was invited to each create an acrostic poem using the word:

C
O
N
N
E
C
T
I
O
N

With a smaller group, a collaborative acrostic could be created using lines from each participant.

An alternative is to invite the group to create list poems, which can be created with pre-provided stems. I have done this with other groups of healthcare staff and students, giving them the following sensory stems, to get them to think differently about what 'connection' means to them:

> The colour of connection is …
> The smell of connection is …
> The texture of connection is …
> The weight of connection is …
> The touch of connection is …

Add on any other lines if you wish to do so. Any word can be used as a stem; with other groups of healthcare staff and students, I have used the words 'resilience', 'belonging', 'community', 'love'. The list is literally endless!

Summary

There are several considerations when working with participants in these groups, but the cornerstone of this work is fostering a safe, confidential and nurturing space for participants to feel comfortable to write and share writing and other issues arising.

It can be hugely satisfying working with others to support them to rediscover/discover their creativity and writing voice, and to be able to offer a way of healing and expression to others in the community, including those receiving healthcare as well as with healthcare and social care staff and students.

ACTIVITY: Writing home

One of my favourite ways of getting writing is to use images as inspiration is Ekphrasis, which means 'description' in Greek. An ekphrastic poem/writing is that inspired by a piece of art, be it visual or music.

Photo by author, June 2018

The concept of home can be a difficult one to articulate – it can include the physical construct (a house, flat, etc.) or a geographical connection, but where is the emotional connection to home? Where do you feel most at home?

a) Freewriting: Using the photo as inspiration, freewrite for five minutes (set a timer); write what comes to you. You may wish to consider the construction and texture of the nests. What is inside the nests? Think about colloquialisms like 'flying the nest' or 'empty nest syndrome'. Does this resonate with you? Use a notebook and pen or pencil rather than a computer or electronic device. Do not stop writing to read back what you have written or to correct spelling. Keep your pen moving across the page.

b) Read your piece and write a poem about what home means to you, incorporating some of these words if you wish.

Works cited and resources:

Beeharry, R. (2021), 'The potentials of creative writing in healthcare education', *Writing in Education,* Issue 83, Spring 2021, p54–55

Beeharry, R. (2023) 'Through the kaleidoscope: creative writing in healthcare education'

https://thepolyphony.org/2023/01/27/through-the-kaleidoscope-creative-writing-in-healthcare-education/

Useful organisations:

Lapidus International is the UK association for those working in the field of writing for wellbeing www.lapidus.org.uk

National Association for Poetry Therapy: www.poetrytherapy.org

Disclosure and Barring Service (DBS):

https://www.gov.uk/government/organisations/disclosure-and-barring-service

Creative Health Quality Framework, Culture, Health & Wellbeing Alliance (2023)

https://www.culturehealthandwellbeing.org.uk/resources/creative-health-quality-framework

Jean Atkin

Writing in the Community

I've been fortunate to have worked as a poet and writer in the community for the last thirteen years, at first in southern Scotland, and then in the West Midlands. My experience has been invigoratingly varied, as I pursued making even a small living. Out of this variety I learned to have confidence in what all sorts of people will write, given the space and the chance, and I've gained in personal happiness and confidence via this sharing in creativity. I've made poems with all sorts of people, of every age – from a two-year-old sitting on a Shire horse: *"he moved and / wobbled me / he was wearing fur // I could see / all the way to his ears"*– to Mary, who lived in a nursing home and at 95 wrote a poem with me about when she was six and watching her own grandmother get dressed: *"First one petticoat, then another, then another, / then another, then another. And I said, how many / do you wear, grandmother? / And she said, only / one more."*

If I had to nail down what my practice is as a jobbing poet, I think it would start with engagement with people. I try to give fresh confidence, and give back confidence that may have been lost along the way. I try to enable, and show how craft can change writing. I love to see someone surprise themselves with what they are able to create. I try to share the notion that writing is about pleasure, can give joy, can be shared. I believe in the democracy of poetry – that it can enhance any life at any time.

Probably because I am a rather outdoors person, it's turned out that quite a lot of my work has been 'outdoors to indoors'. When I was still living in Scotland, I worked with National Scenic Areas, who wanted to draw attention to six specific sites along the Solway coast. We located groups of all ages, and recruited them to walk on the coast, and write some poetry with me about the experience. We created cinquains, a short poetry form based on syllables, which controlled the output. This was essential to the project, as the poems were to be published in small square leaflet form and put into tourist and local information outlets.

I was pretty new to working this way, and learned a lot from this project – not least that for some projects you need to plan for the outcomes and outputs. This project also (like many) required thought about its own marketing, both to recruit the participants and to celebrate their achievements.

Soon after, I spotted that the Scottish Poetry Library, with Creative Scotland, was advertising for four poets to work in Scotland's four botanic gardens, in a project called 'Walking With Poets'. I applied for one of the residencies, registering enthusiastic interest in Logan Botanic Garden and was lucky enough to get the gig.

Staff at the garden wanted me to engage as much as possible with their visitors, encouraging them to explore the garden more deeply. They also wanted publicity for the garden, and to connect its activities and history with contemporary arts. These are very common requirements in a residency, and fair enough! So I gathered a selection of very short poems, some of which were humorous, and I became very practised in rocking up to unsuspecting strangers and offering to share a poem with them. When I could see the whites of their eyes, I'd make a snap decision which poem to read. It was vital, I discovered, to find a rapport with people in the very first moments of conversation. I found this nerve-wracking at first, but I got better! Even so, you have to harden yourself against a minority who are not, no way, going to talk to a poet.

I set up as many activities as I could around the garden, plus a blog. I made a poet tree hung with short poems on red ribbons, I made a garden Dada poetry trail, poetry treasure hunts, led visitors on poetry walks, and offered workshops, both drop-in and pre-booked, on everything from 'Growing a Poem in a Pot' to 'Writing Garden Poetry Postcards'. I was also commissioned to write some poems of my own.

From this experience I was ready to make the next leap. Writing West Midlands guided me through making an Arts Council application to support a residency in Acton Scott Historic Working Farm (by now I was living in Shropshire). As Jonathan Davidson put it to me, "There are lots of places that don't know yet that they need a poet in residence." Such great advice. I approached the farm, sold them the idea and made the application, which fortunately was successful and allowed a summer-long residency. In many ways I used this experience to consolidate and extend what I'd learned in the botanic garden. I approached visitors to the farm, encouraging people of all ages to hear and write poetry in playful, informal settings. Instances of poetry sprouted around the farm buildings and I ran a series of workshops. I worked out of a shepherd's hut, which was great for inviting visitors in and giving them somewhere intriguing to sit while I persuaded them to write poems 'with' me. Doing this made me increasingly skilled at picking out rhythms of speech and personal turns of phrase from what people were saying, and then gathering these into poems that people could recognise themselves in.

The next project was one I organised on my own. I wanted to create a project that was very site-specific, and came up with 'In woods we forget things, at the wood edge we tell stories'.

This project, which was funded by Shropshire Hills AONB (Area of Outstanding Natural Beauty) Conservation Fund and Shropshire Housing Group, provided opportunities for three different groups from the community in south Shropshire to spend time in local native woodlands, learn real, useful conservation skills, respond to place through poetry, and perform their own new site-specific work.

I learned from this that funding to support poetry can be found locally, and also that it's very easy to over-extend yourself! This project demanded a huge amount of time and input from me to support it, and I recklessly promised filming too, because I liked the idea and thought it would help get the funding. Of course then I had to do it, saved only by a teenage son. This was a hugely satisfying project for me, and I loved directing it – but financially, it's fair to say it barely made sense. On the other hand, it helped me to get written into other people's funding bids, something I've been able to rely on much more since then.

Projects and residencies outdoors since then have included 'Impressions of the Past', which offered local people, primary schools and community groups the opportunity to discover, explore and celebrate local Iron Age heritage. I was also fortunate enough to be invited to be 'Troubadour of the Hills' for Ledbury Poetry Festival and Malvern Hills AONB. Other recent outdoors poetry in the community projects have led to me leading workshops on the Long Mynd where we wrote into August darkness by candlelight, and writing in country graveyards, all moths and epitaphs.

Throughout these years, I was learning other ways of writing in the community through working in the care sector. I worked first on a project which put poets into nursing homes in Herefordshire, and was lucky enough to receive a training from renowned dementia poetry practitioner, John Killick.

When that project ended, I had contacts and connections and, until the pandemic, I worked every week in the care sector, with both individuals and groups. Many people of great age are living with some form of dementia, but the groups I worked with frequently contained people with all sorts of disabilities and incapacities. I learned to adapt and respond with sensitivity to whatever the situation seemed to require. So much of this work is about conversation, and listening. I would bring in a poem, or an object and a poem, to start us off. Then we'd talk, and I'd write constant scribbled notes in pencil, trying to capture as much as possible of what people were saying, in their own words. Then I'd read it back to them as a poem, edited on the go. From this, I realised the experience of making a collaborative poem together was hugely bonding for a group, and the care homes told me how friendships within the groups were deepening as a result. I found it moving to capture the words of these elders, who would in these sessions discuss death, and the length of their lives, with such grace. And we laughed a lot.

I've also worked extensively in schools, mostly primary and middle. Sometimes I have no particular brief, and sometimes I'm asked to fit what I do to a curriculum theme. It is as well to plan carefully and provide children with clear instructions and restrictions – this will actually help them to be creative, rather than not. Finding (or writing) a poem for inspiration and using it to 'scaffold' their own writing is a reliable way in.

I use my techniques for making collaborative 'instant' poems with them too, as it leads them into their own writing in a risk-free way, and helps children who are expressive but, for example, dyslexic, to have their voices heard and appreciated. When I make an instant collaborative poem, I share with the children my thinking about finding a good last line, or a good refrain line, or a place where something different starts to happen in the poem. We talk about line endings, and white space. I play games with them to generate unexpected imagery.

I've also developed lots of warm-ups and fillers to use in classrooms – there's often five minutes at some point, or a moment when everyone needs a lift and a change. Managing the time you have is a big part of working in a school, where often I find I'm timetabled to see as many classes as they can squash in. One school merrily timetabled me right through lunch …

Another place to work is with libraries, archives and museums. In this sector there is so much marvellous material – but usually near non-existent budgets. Sometimes I've wangled a fee from a different project and 'spent' it in the museum, and more often I've offered a series of workshops for which participants pay me direct. In this way, I've worked with curators, archivists and the Regional Finds Officer, who brought in actual Saxon gold to show to my group so we could write about it.

Poetry in the community can be about playful spectacle and visibility, and I had this in mind when I invented The Spellwright. The Spellwright is poetry-theatre, for which I don a big medieval frock and sit behind a table embellished with skulls, huge pine cones, live snails and a wooden doll. The public come to find out what it's all about, and then I invite them to write a spell with me. I ask them "What would make your life better?" As a result, I've written spells for health, happiness, wings, an end to inequality, the ability to walk through walls, talk to owls, send a baby to sleep, and get a man out of a bar (which worked instantly). I work with brown stained paper, a steel dip pen, calligraphy ink, sealing wax, brass stamp and candle. The Spellwright has appeared at festivals and events, libraries, schools, hospitals and day centres. She's happy to work indoors or outdoors as she has a good wool cloak. I enjoy her enormously and, so far, no-one has ever requested a spell for cash. Though someone did once ask for a hex, which I thoughtfully declined to produce.

Finally, there is also the online community. When the pandemic hit, I created The Poetry Wire, a series of six-week themed online courses around a website available only to participants. I provide writing prompts, and detailed written feedback on one poem per week per participant and, when they've edited it, I upload it on The Poetry Wire where it can be read by others on the course. They can comment on each other's work, and once a week we hold a celebratory Zoom session to share readings of that week's new work. I find this very intensive to teach, but very satisfying.

To conclude, I have had the best working time of my life taking poetry into the community, and there's lots of room for more of us to do so. I wish you luck and many fresh words!

ACTIVITY: A way to make poetry public

Approach a local-to-you event, and offer to provide small poems to the public, perhaps using the event or festival's theme.

Your poems could be written in advance, just two-liners either to keep, or to pass on guerrilla-poetry-style. Or you could be brave and offer to write very small poems (use small pieces of nice paper or card) on the spot.

People like to have something to take away with them. They can be handwritten or typed on a portable typewriter (good because it's visual, and nowadays vintage and cute). Tie things up with ribbon? Use sealing wax?

Consider making yourself a large sign to explain what you're up to so that every conversation doesn't start from scratch. Make it playful, make it easy to walk up to.

Jane Commane

Standing in the Rain Together: Why We Should Take Poetry Out into the World

Picture the scene – it's 2008 and I am at an outdoor summer festival in a city in the midlands. Bands are playing on the main stage, the atmosphere is buzzing. The clouds are darkening though, and suddenly the heavens open and crowds start making for the indoor stages. I'm near the entrance to one big-top tent as one stream of soaked festival-goers make their way in for shelter. But as they do, there's a pause in the flow – and within a few minutes, the torrent of people *in* becomes a steady flow back *out* again. One man stops another on his way in to say, "I wouldn't go in there if I were you. They're doing *poetry*." Accompanied by groans of dismay, a steady stream of festival-goers head back out into the rain.

It's a moment I often think back to; and I share it not to be judgemental of that audience or their reaction, but just to remind myself that poetry, no matter how immersed I have been in it and all the magic it holds for me, is still sometimes trapped by its own stereotypes for some; dull, worthy, boring – annoying even – worth avoiding, worse than getting a soaking. And also to remind myself that poetry can also be anything but – it can be invigorating, deeply moving, unforgettable, laugh-out-loud funny, heartbreaking, unifying and powerful. And for me, how much it matters to be a lightning conductor for this transference of energy as a poet – to share *that* sort of poetry reaction with more people in the hope that they too might experience poetry in all its electrifying wonder for themselves.

***

Much has changed since that day in the mid 2000s. Poetry possesses a great deal more hybridity, diversity, and innovation than ever before as an artform. There's much more for everyone to find something which they may enjoy, or which might speak to them. There's also a deeper crossover between page and performance, and so much more cross-pollination between poetry and digital, spoken, film, visual and musical artforms. But still, many people will not yet have encountered this, and may still feel put off by the *idea* of poetry.

Perhaps these misgivings we have, when we think poetry isn't for us, is something to do with where we first encounter poetry formally. For many, this may well be in secondary school, where a little like algebra or chemical equations, it becomes something we have to learn to analyse and solve, find the answers for, and be tested on. We may end up only learning to detest it, unless we're fortunate enough to have teachers who love poetry and put their enthusiasm into teaching it well and breaking down our resistance to it and some of poetry's innate resistance to us. There is in that idea of *resistance* the suggestion of a kind of 'mysterious' knowledge being required to understand poetry – a knowledge that is perhaps withheld and which requires a specific key to unlock. Believing we don't have this – or permission for it – we may well feel locked out of what poetry is meant to do for us.

For some, there may still be the trappings of class and privilege that hangs over poetry – the idea that like much of what is sometimes regarded 'high' art rather than popular culture, it 'belongs' to a set of people with a certain educational background, who have the key to understanding it. We may think *It's not for the likes of us. It isn't ours.*

And so, disenfranchised from the culture of poetic language, we come to believe that it belongs in that rarefied place. Or perhaps that it is, like that mouldering bottle of sherry in the sideboard, for special occasions or emergency use only; in births, deaths and marriages – or exam papers. Out of reach, in its special little box.

***

Informally, however, we really encounter poetry well before that: in the chime of names and words, then the nursery rhymes we hear when tucked in at night, the fairy stories and counting songs we learn from the parquet floors of reception class, words of spells, blessing or prayer, the old pop ballads our parents might sing over the washing up. Into our ears all those lovely looping rhythmic language sounds – precious and part of us as we grow, imbibed into our blood and bones. The words we ask for again and again, the ones that make us feel at home, that we belong. We will remember much of it all our lives. Here, the language and work of poetry is innately all around us.

So let me propose this: what if we awaken and attune ourselves to language and the work of poetry again; begin to notice the experience of it as part of our everyday, just as naturally as we did when we were young, without drawing for ourselves the borders of special knowledge or permission?

What if we start to fall back in love with it all – from the accidental poetry of speech and rhythm, through to lyrics we overhear, the snippets of text and accidental poetry in signs, posters and found texts, to the little silent lines of thought as we go out into the world and, language itself translates our senses and perception?

Suddenly poetry breaks free from its box on a high shelf. It becomes everywhere, belonging to everybody, and no one, all at once.

And what if we seek to awaken and kindle that love of words in others, too?

What if we find ways to make poetry appear in our day-to-day lives, and no more shrink from it than we would a beautiful hand-drawn card or an irresistibly catchy song?

And in taking poetry out of its box, you create the chance meeting, where poetry might just meet its new biggest fan.

And I realise this is why taking poetry out into the world for new encounters – through a whole host of surprising, fun, and innovative ways – really matters.

***

For poets, I think the question of *how* and *why* we could take poetry out into the world, and how we encourage others to access, read, hear, and return to poetry is a fundamentally fascinating and multifaceted one. I have no single answer as to *how* to do this – there are so many possible ways to for poetry to find its way into our common shared culture, and I will suggest a few ways to begin approaching the *how* in just a moment. But for now, let's just consider a few of the *whys*.

Why? I want for more people to find what I have found in poetry, from childhood and all my days since: connection, the process that anchors something felt into words, the sensation of still reaching towards something not yet quite fully understood. A burning fuse. An impelling force like life itself. As quoted in *Detectorists*: "My heart has followed all my days – Something I cannot name!" (Don Marquis).

Why? Not that poetry can be fully analysed and understood and put away, but rather that it cannot – and it holds yet so much more for us to unravel.

Why? Because we live in age where, as writer Elif Shafak observes, "in which there is too much information, less knowledge and even less wisdom. That ratio needs to be reversed" (*How to Stay Sane in an Age of Division*). Whilst we absorb huge amounts of information, we are also drained, exhausted, and battered by much of it. Language is often twisted and abused by those with power. It can be manipulated to make us feel sad, worthless, envious, or divided. And yet poetry has the power to restore for us that which is valuable about language: that there is something wise, precious, solace-giving or thought-provoking we may find in it.

Why? Because poetry can give us the words for things we may not yet have processed or been able to approach. It makes us feel less alone. It gives us new ways to see and understand. It creates a radical space of empathy. It can start conversations, bridge gaps. A poem has potential to make a common ground in the four walls of its words.

***

But let me come back down to earth from my giddiness about poetry's possibilities for a moment, to be practicalities of *how* to take poetry out into the world and share it with others.

I also feel it's important to add we should be conscious, in all our excitement, not to force poetry onto people who may not want, need, or feel ready for poems yet, and not be judgemental of anyone who says *No thank you – not for me*. We don't have to enjoy *everything*, and we shouldn't expect others to either.

Perhaps the best way we approach this as poets is to see our situation more as envoys, ambassadors to poetry – whose role is sharing and opening poetry to the world, rather than trying to make the world pay attention to poetry. If we change our perspective and think about poetry as a gift we can invite people to partake from if they'd like to, it becomes less focused on the 'musts' and 'shoulds' of reaction, and more on the possibility of encounters.

For us as poets, this may mean saying less – 'I will now read you a poem and you must stand here and look like it did something for you' and more 'oh look, here's a poem someone printed and displayed instead of an advert on the bus', or 'here's a poem someone read aloud on a podcast and I wasn't expecting it there, but actually really enjoyed it' or 'I saw this poem on the pinboard at work. I read it whilst eating my Pot Noodle. It wasn't too bad. I'd do that again' (the poem, maybe, as well as the Pot Noodle).

It may involve less expectation of 'Poems' with a capital P to be produced or read or heard and certified as enjoyed – and all the pressure that may entail. And instead, more about having fun with language that builds into one big communal poem which turns into something unexpectedly moving as everyone recognises their own words as part of the whole at the end. It may involve asking questions. It'll definitely involve listening, scribing, highlighting – finding the sparkle of gold in our everyday experiences and words.

And by this gentle, curious, and open sharing, and holding up to the light, we as writers can play a role of embedding poetry into the fabric of our culture more intrinsically, of making the language of poetry something we are more likely to encounter ordinarily rather than exceptionally. That maybe it no longer becomes something we'd stand in the rain to avoid.

***

As the essays in this book amply demonstrate, if you're keen to take poetry out into the world, there are many cheap, simple ways you can do it yourself, by yourself – as well as ways you can advance, learn new skills, and be well-equipped to go a little further.

For instance, you might decide to make a mini poetry pamphlet to leave in waiting rooms with a 'Take Me' note on. Or design some poster-poems to cheer up noticeboards and hallways. You could even approach a local bookshop or library and ask if you could make bespoke poem-bookmarks for visitors or customers. It doesn't have to be your own poems you share; it could be an old favourite which is out of copyright. You could even ask a poet or publisher if they will allow you to share a poem in this way, if you make clear how you intend to share it. If you do leave a little trail of poems behind you, take care not to litter anywhere or use plastics or other materials that won't biodegrade.

If you're into technology or have other strings to your creative bow, like film, visual arts or music, then you now know that poetry can be a perfect partner. Interesting things happen when we start to mix things up; it also creates the possibility of new audiences finding poetry in a new context. Live performance, and creating poetry in theatre or performance spaces, is also another way to spread the word of poetry and create chance-meetings with new audiences as a result.

Or you may hope to find yourself doing the direct work of being a poet in public, and working with groups, communities or organisations, and using poetry as a way to connect, create space and forge new conversations or experiences. It's a great way to share poems and make new ones together. Think about how those poems your group make can be further shared and transmitted – can they be broadcast or printed, filmed? – could they even go on a billboard or on posters with the help of train or bus companies, or printed onto a local shop's paper bags or made into badges or t-shirts and become wearable poems?

What matters most is that you don't have to do **all** of these things to take poetry out into the world. We all have different confidence and comfort levels, and specific skills that may lend themselves to different areas and approaches. Give some consideration to what feels right for you – and what you have experience in. Don't be afraid to ask to shadow someone and get some first-hand experience if you'd like to know more about how others take poetry out into the world in various ways.

And more than anything, the best way is to remind yourself what first made you love poetry, and to find a way you can continue to honour and share that love.

***

Having inspired you to see poetry as a brilliant thing to carry out into the world, here are a few practical and creative considerations to bear in mind:

Let it be slippery: Don't worry too much about 'is this poetry?' at the early stages. Put words, sentences, images, metaphors, and ideas out into the world. Fragments can be every bit as powerful and immediate as a fully-formed poem. Allow yourself to cross-pollinate other artforms – visual poems, sound poems, film poems.

Keep it cheap and DIY: And teach yourself new things along the way. You don't need to spend lots of money on expensive kit or tech to start with. Begin with what you have. Use online tutorials. Hand-make things and do a few things for free to test what works. learn to embrace making and creating and sometimes failing as part of the process.

Make no assumptions: People have a great capacity for understanding and taking leaps of faith where language and poetry is concerned. Don't make assumptions about what they'll enjoy or over-simplify or flummox people with poetry. Just try and share things you truly love and be passionate about them. Be open to people not liking or enjoying them as much as you do. Be curious and maybe ask what they *do* like or remember of poetry.

Don't be afraid to let go: The work your produce as part of collaborations, or for specific commissions and projects doesn't have to be your greatest ever work. It can sit a little alongside your main poetry portfolio. Open it up to possibility, write in ways you wouldn't normally, use poetic forms or let it flow as fragments, ideas, snippets. Be less precious, but don't be less adventurous – you can still make things that are challenging and thoughtful.

Make sure it fits well with you: If you're approached to work on a project or collaboration where you feel either yourself or your work isn't that well understood, or that the organisation, or fellow artists haven't thought the engagement or creative elements through fully, it's fine to walk away. Scrutinise the skills the project needs – if it involves working with a group or in a specific space or framework where you feel inexperienced or underprepared, then maybe it isn't right for you. There will be poets for whom this is *exactly* their thing though – so do a good turn, and recommend them if you turn it down.

You don't have to do everything: There are a plethora of brilliant projects you can be involved with or create yourself – and this book is of course only a snapshot. But it's vital to know yourself as a poet and as a facilitator of projects, and to know, honestly, where your skills and time are best employed. Learn what works for you and if you enjoy it, so will those you encounter.

Listen and be Curious: Ask questions and be interested in what people you're encountering have to say about poetry and language. Give them your time. Use poetry to open doors, don't instruct on how poems *should* or *must* be received or understood. It isn't a classroom and there's no right response – just the opportunity for possibilities, for a poem to meet someone halfway. It might just change their life – and sometimes poems do.

***

To end where we began, come back with me to that same midlands city. It's November 2019 and (inevitably) raining again.

Over three nights, 15,000 people come out into the drizzle to stand in the ruins of Coventry Cathedral and watch and listen to the sound and light installation which features a poem I've been commissioned to write collaboratively with school children and community groups in the city. It's for a project with Historic England and the Poetry Society – *Where Light Falls* – which tells the story of those who risked their lives to protect the cathedral during wartime, its destruction and postwar reconstruction.

An evocative music score, composed for the poem, fills the night air. A light show moves from a galaxy of medieval stained-glass to red flames and ruins, to shades of Coventry blue, projected 284 metres high onto the spire of St Michael's. Crowds fill the open-air ruins and gaze upwards to watch the performances throughout the evening. Some have come across it by accident on the way home from work or study; others return the next night to share the experience with family and friends. It's an intense and often very moving experience to watch people watching it.

Even if I never write another poem, I'll always be proud of this one – written as a gift for the city I was born in, and for its people, which found so many who were willing to receive it.

This time, we're standing in the rain together – and all around us is poetry.

ACTIVITY: Poetry as gift

Why not give a favourite or treasured poem you've loved and appreciated over the years as a gift to someone? A poem shared and passed on is a wonderful way to continue the journey of a poem we've previously enjoyed and cherished, which has spoken to us or holds special meaning.

You might want to write up the poem on a card in your own handwriting with a good fountain pen – writing out a poem is also a good way of committing it to ourselves.

Wrap it up or put it inside an envelope. Write it onto the reverse of a postcard, or maybe even frame it so it so that it can be hung on the wall or kept as a keepsake.

Further Reading

'How to' guides:

52: Write a Poem a Week. Start Now. Keep Going – Jo Bell and guest poets (Nine Arches Press, 2015).

How to be a Poet: A 21ˢᵗ Century Guide to Writing Well – Jo Bell and Jane Commane (Nine Arches Press, 2017).

The Craft: A Guide to Making Poetry Happen in the 21st Century – ed. Rishi Dastidar (Nine Arches Press, 2019).

Why I Write Poetry – ed. Ian Humphreys (Nine Arches Press, 2021).

Cambridge Introduction to Creative Writing – David Morley (Cambridge Introductions to Literature, 2011).

An Introduction to English Poetry – James Fenton (Penguin, 2003)

The Practice of Poetry: Writing Exercises From Poets Who Teach – eds. Robin Behn, Chase Twichell (William Morrow Paperbacks, 1992).

Writing Poems – Peter Sansom (Bloodaxe, 1993).

Writing Poetry – W. N. Herbert (Routledge, 2009).

Essay collections:

Stress Fractures: Essays on Poetry – ed. Tom Chivers (Penned in the Margins, 2010).

The Redress of Poetry – Seamus Heaney (Faber & Faber, 2002).

Madness, Rack, and Honey: Collected Lectures – Mary Ruefle (Wave Books, 2012).

Don't Ask Me What I Mean: Poets in Their Own Words – eds. Don Paterson and Clare Brown (Picador, 2012).

In Their Own Words: Contemporary Poets on their Poetry – eds. Helen Ivory and George Szirtes (Salt Publishing, 2012).

On Poetry – Glyn Maxwell (Oberon Books, 2012/2017).

Strong Words: Modern Poets on Modern Poetry – eds. W. N. Herbert and Matthew Hollis (Bloodaxe, 2000).

More inspiration:

Nobody Knows What They're Doing: The 10 Secrets All Artists Should Know – Lee Crutchley (St Martin's Press, 2021).

Poetry And Dementia: A Practical Guide – John Killick (St Martin's Press, 2017).

The Artist's Way: A Spiritual Path to Higher Creativity – Julia Cameron (Profile Books, 2020).

The Gift: How the Creative Spirit Transforms the World – Lewis Hyde (Canongate, 2022).

On Poetry – Jonathan Davidson (Smith I Doorstop, 2018).

#Afterhours – Inua Ellams (Nine Arches Press, 2017).

Biographies

Deborah Alma is a poet, editor and bookseller. She was the Emergency Poet, offering poetry on prescription from her vintage ambulance. She co-founded the world's first walk-in Poetry Pharmacy in 2019. She is editor of *Emergency Poet: an anti-stress poetry anthology, #MeToo rallying against sexual harassment, The National Trust Book of Nature Poems* and co-editor of *These Are the Hands – Poems from the Heart of the NHS*. Her collection *Dirty Laundry* is published by Nine Arches Press.

Jean Atkin has been a poet in education and community projects since 2011. Her third full collection, *High Nowhere*, is forthcoming from IDP. She has worked with many organisations, including Meadow Arts, English Heritage, the Arvon Foundation and Ledbury Poetry Festival. She has led out-of-doors twilight workshops and has been BBC Poet for Shropshire for National Poetry Day. www.jeanatkin.com

Casey Bailey is a Birmingham-born writer and educator. Casey's award-winning work spans multiple spaces, from poetry to theatre, music to education. Casey's poetry is widely published and commissioned, and has been performed internationally. He is a fellow of the University of Worcester and in 2021 was awarded an Honorary Doctorate in Education by Newman University.

Roshni Beeharry is a writer, Medical Educator, Writing for Wellbeing Facilitator (www.storiedselves.com) and former doctor. Her writing is published internationally, including in *Litro, Writers' Magazine, Atrium Press, Tendon* and *These are the Hands* anthology. Roshni was longlisted for the Aeon Prize, highly commended in the Hippocrates Prize for Poetry & Medicine, and a finalist in Cuirt Literary Festival competition.

Jo Bell is one of the UK's best respected poetry coaches, teaching for the Arvon Foundation, the Writing School and others. Her award-winning online communities include the 52 project, which changed the UK poetry landscape, and now 'slow poetry' forum The Poetic Licence which encourages the lifelong enjoyment of writing. Her own poetry has won major awards. She hosts the podcast Three Poems and a Question.

Julia Bird is a poet and producer who grew up in Gloucestershire and now lives in London. She has worked for poetry organisations, including the Poetry Book Society, the Poetry School and The Poetry Society. Through her company Jaybird Live Literature, she has produced eight touring live literature shows. Her poetry publications are *Hannah and the Monk* (Salt Publishing, 2008), *Twenty-Four Seven Blossom* (Salt Publishing, 2013), *Now You Can Look* (The Emma Press, 2017), *Paper Trail* (with Mike Sims, Blown Rose, 2019), *is, thinks Pearl* (The Emma Press, 2021) and *A Joy Forever: a walk out with John Keats* (with Mike Sims, Paekakariki Press, 2021). @juliamarybird

Jane Burn is a working-class, pansexual, essayist, poet, artist, and person with autism. Her work has been widely published and anthologised and she has an MA in Writing Poetry from Newcastle University. Her latest collection, *Be Feared*, is available from Nine Arches Press. She lives off-grid with her family in a Northumberland cottage for most of the year.

Born in 1993, **Lewis Buxton** is a writer and theatre maker. His work has appeared in *The Independent, Poetry Review, The Rialto,* and *Magma* amongst others. His first collection *Boy in Various Poses* was published by Nine Arches Press in 2021. His debut theatre show 'BOY!' is on tour in 2023. He lives in Norfolk.

Jane Commane's poetry has featured in *Staying Human* (Bloodaxe), *The Guardian, Butcher's Dog* and *Poetry Birmingham Literary Journal.* In 2016, she was selected for Writing West Midlands' Room 204 development programme and awarded a Jerwood Compton Poetry Fellowship in 2017. Her collection, *Assembly Lines* (Bloodaxe, 2018) was longlisted for the Michael Murphy Memorial Prize. Jane is director and editor at Nine Arches Press.

Jonathan Davidson is Chief Executive of Writing West Midlands, in which capacity he has completed many funding applications. He writes here in a personal capacity. www.writingwestmidlands.org

Helen Dewbery is a poetry filmmaker whose works, curations and talks have been presented at festivals and exhibitions in the UK and internationally. Teaching is an integral part of her practice, enabling people's own capacity, and sharing the practical and technical skills of poetry filmmaking, alongside conceptual and critical engagement. She is editor of the online magazine www.poetryfilmlive.com.

Pat Edwards is a writer, reviewer and workshop leader from mid Wales. She hosts Verbatim open mic nights and curates Welshpool Poetry Festival. Her work has appeared in *Magma, Prole, Atrium, IS&T*, as well as in anthologies. Pat has three pamphlets: *Only Blood* (Yaffle, 2019), *Kissing in the Dark* (Indigo Dreams, 2020) and *Hail Marys* (Infinity Books UK, 2022).

Jasmine Gardosi is the Birmingham Poet Laureate. Her work has appeared on Button Poetry, PBS, BBC and Sky Arts. She is a multiple slam champion, beatboxer, winner of the Out-Spoken Prize for Poetry and the Saboteur Award for Best Spoken Word Performer. Her award-winning show about gender identity, 'Dancing To Music You Hate', combines poetry, beatbox and Celtic dubstep.

Roz Goddard is a poet and teacher. Her poetry collection, *Lost City* (The Emma Press), was published in 2020. Previous short collections have been published by Nine Arches Press and Flarestack Poets. She was a finalist for the Moth Poetry Prize in 2022 and works as a poetry mentor for The Poetry Society. Her forthcoming collection, *Small Moon Curve*, will be published in 2024 (Nine Arches Press). She is currently training for ordination in the Triratna Buddhist Order. She is a former poet laureate of Birmingham.

Daisy Henwood is a writer and arts producer based in Norwich. Her work has appeared in *The Rialto, Poetry Wales, Poetry Birmingham Literary Journal,* and *Under the Radar*. She received her PhD from UEA in 2020. She was writer-in-residence at Norwich Castle in 2021 and virtual writer-in-residence at the Werribee River Association, Melbourne, in 2022.

Sophie Herxheimer's work has been shown at Tate Modern, The Migration Museum, and along the sea-front at Margate. She's made a 300 metre tablecloth for the Thames Festival, devised the colour palette for Cbeebies In the Night Garden, and held residencies from Corby to California. One recent collection is *INDEX* (zimZalla, 2021) 78 cut up poems, published as a tarot deck.

Helen Ivory edits *Ink, Sweat & Tears* and teaches online for UEA/ NCW. *Wunderkammer,* her *New and Selected Poems* was published by MadHat (US) in 2022. She has work translated into Polish, Ukrainian, Spanish, Croatian and Greek, for Versopolis. She is working on her sixth Bloodaxe Books collection *Constructing a Witch* (2024). She is also a visual artist and makes collage poems and shadowboxes.

Gregory Leadbetter's books and pamphlets of poetry include *Caliban* (Dare-Gale Press, 2023), *Balanuve,* with photographs by Phil Thomson (Broken Sleep Books, 2021), *Maskwork* (Nine Arches Press, 2020), *The Fetch* (Nine Arches Press, 2016), and *The Body in the Well* (HappenStance Press, 2007). He is Professor of Poetry at Birmingham City University.

Arji Manuelpillai is a poet, performer and facilitator based in London. Arji's debut pamphlet *Mutton Rolls* was published with Out-Spoken Press in 2020 and his newest book *Improvised Explosive Device* was released in the Autumn of 2022 with Penned in the Margins. This highly acclaimed book was the Winter PBS selection and shortlisted for the Derek Walcott Prize.

Caleb Parkin, Bristol City Poet 2020 - 22, has poems in numerous journals and anthologies, tutoring, facilitating and mentoring for Arvon, Poetry Society, Poetry School and elsewhere. He's published three pamphlets and a collection, *This Fruiting Body* (Nine Arches, longlisted Laurel Prize). He holds an MSc Creative Writing for Therapeutic Purposes; from 2023 he's a practice-as-research PhD candidate at University of Exeter, as part of RENEW Biodiversity.

Nina Mingya Powles is a writer, zinemaker and librarian from Aotearoa New Zealand, currently living in London. She is the author of several poetry pamphlets, zines and poetry books, most recently *Magnolia* 木蘭, *Tiny Moons: A Year of Eating in Shanghai,* and a collection of essays, *Small Bodies of Water.* She is a pamphlet selector for the Poetry Book Society in the UK, and writes an occasional e-newsletter on food and memory called Crispy Noodles.

Jacqueline Saphra's second collection, *All My Mad Mothers* (Nine Arches Press, 2017) was shortlisted for the TS Eliot Prize and her fifth, *Velvel's Violin,* a Poetry Book Society Recommendation, was published by Nine Arches Press in July 2023. She is a founder member of Poets for the Planet and teaches for The Poetry School.

Clare Shaw (they/them) has four poetry collections with Bloodaxe. Their latest collection *Towards a General Theory of Love* (2022) is a poetic interrogation of love and its absence: it attracted a Northern Writer's Award, and was a Poetry Society Book of the Year 2022. Clare lectures at the University of Huddersfield, and is a regular tutor for Wordsworth Grasmere, the Royal Literary Fund and the Arvon Foundation. With a background in mental health and education, Clare is a keen advocate for writing as means of personal and social change.

Degna Stone is a poet and poetry editor based in northeast England. They are a contributing editor at *The Rialto* and a co-founder of *Butcher's Dog* poetry magazine. Their debut full-length collection *Proof of Life on Earth* was published by Nine Arches Press in November 2022.

Tamar Yoseloff's sixth collection is *The Black Place* (Seren, 2019). She's also the author of *Formerly* (with photographs by Vici MacDonald), shortlisted for the Ted Hughes Award, and collaborative editions with artists Linda Karshan and Charlotte Harker respectively. Her upcoming collection, *Belief Systems*, is due from Nine Arches Press in 2024. She works as a freelance lecturer in creative writing.